PRAYERS THAT DESTROY DEMONS FROM THE UNDERGROUND WORLD

STARIA MIELKE

EDITED BY

NICOLE QUEEN

VISION PUBLISHING
HOUSE

Vision Publishing House
support@vision-publishinghouse.com
www.vision-publishinghouse.com

ISBN: 979-8-9933667-4-6 (print)
LCCN: 2025923459

To those who have felt oppressed, attacked, or bound by spiritual forces beyond their control—may you find freedom, healing, and divine protection through the prayers and strategies in this book.

I have given you authority to trample on snakes and scorpions and to overcome all the power of the enemy; nothing will harm you.

— LUKE 10:19 (NIV)

CONTENTS

PART FIVE
TARGETED PRAYERS

PART SIX
ANCHORED IN PRAYER

PART SEVEN
RESOURCES FOR GROWTH

INTRODUCTION

Throughout history, prayer has served as a powerful weapon for protection, healing, and spiritual warfare. This book is a divine assignment, given to me by the Lord, to equip believers with prayers that combat and destroy demonic forces operating from the underground world. These prayers are not just words; they are spiritual weapons designed to empower individuals, families, ministries, and entire communities.

The Spirit of God revealed to me that this book would help many five-fold ministry leaders return to their rightful place in the church, actively engaging in the demonstration of miracles, signs, and wonders through healing and deliverance. As I write these words, I give all the glory to God for anointing me to compile this book, which is intended to strengthen you in your ministry and equip you for spiritual battle.

In *Prayers That Destroy Demons*, the Holy Spirit has inspired me to reveal strategies that will enable you to break demonic forces from your life, family, home, spouse, children, ministry, and beyond. I encourage you to pay close attention to every detail, as the revelations contained within this book will open realms and dimensions of divine manifestations in these 'end times.'

On June 13, 2020, the Lord instructed me to write down these teachings as He guided me on how to fast, pray, and war against underground demonic forces. While many may dismiss the existence of such entities, the spiritual realm is real, and its impact can manifest in the natural world. Through the Holy Spirit's guidance, I will expose hidden strategies of the enemy and provide you with the necessary prayers to overcome them.

Some of the key revelations in this book include:

- *Breaking Witchcraft Codes:* Understanding the significance of numbers, dates, and sequences used by witches and warlocks to establish demonic strongholds.

- *Destroying Evil Altars:* Recognizing and dismantling spiritual altars where rituals and spells are performed.

- *Deliverance from Spiritual Attacks:* Engaging in effective prayers to break free from the influence of curses, amulets, voodoo, and occult practices.

This book is a divine strategy, a war manual for believers who are ready to take authority over the forces of darkness. Let's begin this journey together—one of knowledge, power, and victory in Jesus Christ.

HOW TO USE THIS BOOK

This book is not meant to be read passively but actively engaged with. Spiritual warfare requires persistence, faith, and strategic application of the Word of God. Below are some guidelines to help you maximize the effectiveness of this book in your personal or ministry prayer life.

1. Pray with Expectation and Authority

Each prayer in this book is rooted in biblical principles and inspired by the Holy Spirit. When you pray, do so with faith, believing that God will move on your behalf. Declare the words with boldness, standing on the promises of Scripture.

2. Fast and Consecrate Yourself as Led

Fasting is a powerful spiritual discipline that strengthens prayer and intensifies spiritual breakthroughs. Seek the Lord's guidance on when and how to incorporate fasting into your spiritual warfare.

3. Apply the Scriptures

Throughout this book, you will find warfare prayers accompanied by relevant Scriptures. These verses serve as the foundation for your prayers and should be declared regularly. Meditate on them, memorize them, and use them as spiritual weapons against the enemy.

4. Remain Consistent in Prayer

Deliverance and spiritual breakthroughs often require persistence. Some prayers may need to be repeated over days, weeks, or even months. Stay steadfast in your faith, knowing that God's timing is perfect.

5. Create a Prayer Schedule

Consider setting aside dedicated times to pray through specific sections of the book. Whether it's morning intercession, midnight warfare, or corporate prayer with a group, structure your prayer time to maintain discipline in spiritual warfare.

6. Be Led by the Holy Spirit

While this book provides structured prayers, always allow the Holy Spirit to guide you. He may reveal specific areas in your life that need deliverance or give you unique strategies to combat spiritual attacks.

7. Guard Your Heart and Mind

Spiritual warfare can be intense, and the enemy may attempt to counterattack. Stay rooted in God's presence by maintaining a lifestyle of worship, gratitude, and faith. Surround yourself with fellow believers who can intercede with you and encourage you in your journey.

8. Use This Book for Personal and Corporate Prayer

This book is designed for individual believers, intercessors, pastors, and prayer warriors. Whether you use it for personal deliverance, church prayer groups, or ministry training, apply the prayers in alignment with the Word of God.

* * *

As you journey through this book, remember that victory belongs to the Lord. Jesus Christ has already conquered the powers of darkness, and through Him, we have authority to trample upon serpents and scorpions (Luke 10:19). Stand firm in your faith, walk in the power of God, and watch as strongholds are broken and miracles manifest in your life.

Let us now move forward into this spiritual warfare journey, armed and ready to destroy the works of darkness in Jesus' name.

PART ONE
EQUIPPED FOR BATTLE

Before confronting the spirit of darkness, you must first be fortified by the Holy Spirit. Therefore, this section is your spiritual training ground—designed to prepare your heart, sharpen your discernment, and awaken your authority through prayer.

Here, you will explore the power and purpose of prayer in spiritual warfare, discover how to fast with intention, and learn how to invoke heaven's help through intercession, worship, and Scripture. You'll be equipped not just to survive battles—but to win them with boldness, clarity, and the fire of the Holy Spirit.

Let this wisdom serve as your armor before the confrontation. The war is real—but so is your authority.

CHAPTER ONE
THE POWER OF PRAYER

Prayer is more than a religious routine—it is a divine lifeline that connects heaven and earth. In the life of the believer, prayer is not just communication; it is transformation. It is where burdens are lifted, clarity is received, and battles are won before they ever manifest in the natural realm. Whether whispered through tears or shouted in faith, every sincere prayer moves the heart of God.

In this chapter, we will explore the many dimensions of prayer—its comfort, power, and supernatural ability to shape outcomes, fortify your spirit, and anchor you in God's presence.

THE IMPACT OF PRAYER IN SPIRITUAL BATTLE

The impact of prayer can be understood in various ways, depending on one's beliefs, experiences, and cultural context. Here are some perspectives on its significance:

1. *Spiritual Connection:* For many, prayer is a way to connect

with a higher power or divine entity. It can foster a sense of relationship with the sacred.

2. *Comfort and Peace:* Prayer often provides comfort during difficult times, helping individuals find peace, hope, and strength in challenging circumstances.

3. *Community and Support:* Praying together can create a sense of community and solidarity among individuals. It fosters connections and support networks.

4. *Mindfulness and Reflection:* Engaging in prayer can serve as a form of meditation, allowing practitioners to reflect on their lives, intentions, and emotions, promoting mental well-being.

5. *Positive Psychology:* Studies in psychology suggest that prayer can lead to improved mental health outcomes, including lower levels of anxiety and depression, increased optimism, and resilience.

6. *Manifesting Intentions:* Some believe that prayer can help manifest intentions or desires in life. This belief often ties into the concept of the law of attraction.

Ultimately, the power of prayer varies greatly among individuals. It can be a deeply personal and transformative practice that encompasses a wide range of emotions and experiences.

THE ROLE OF PRAYER IN SPIRITUAL BATTLE

When you enter spiritual warfare, you're not just confronting visible problems—you're challenging invisible principalities. In these unseen realms, prayer is your greatest weapon. Throughout history, believers have used prayer to pull down strongholds, silence demonic voices, and release divine intervention. This chapter explores how prayer functions as a spiritual strategy—one rooted in biblical authority and empowered by faith.

As you read, you'll uncover historical examples, scriptural truths, and personal testimonies that show just how vital prayer is when confronting darkness and securing victory. Below are some instances and perspectives that highlight this relationship:

1. Biblical Examples

- Jesus' Exorcisms: In the New Testament, Jesus frequently used prayer and commands to cast out demons. For instance, in Mark 1:23-26, Jesus encounters a man possessed by an unclean spirit and simply commands the spirit to leave, illustrating the authority of prayer and the spoken word in spiritual conflict.

- The Temptation of Jesus: In Matthew 4:1-11, Jesus fasts and prays in the wilderness before facing Satan's temptations. His reliance on Scripture during these encounters exemplifies prayer as a foundation of spiritual strength.

2. The Early Church

- The Apostles and Prayer: Early Christians often gathered for prayer, asking for God's intervention in times of persecution and spiritual challenges (Acts 4:23-31). Their collective prayers are recorded as being powerful enough to shake the foundations of the place where they met, signifying a communal spiritual battle against oppressive forces.

3. *Historical Saints and Figures*

- St. Francis of Assisi: Known for his deep devotion to prayer and the spiritual life, St. Francis reportedly engaged in prayers of exorcism, believing in the power of prayer to overcome darkness.

- St. Teresa of Ávila: In her writings on prayer and contemplation, she noted how prayer serves as a means of spiritual warfare, helping believers resist temptation and demonic influence.

4. *The Reformation Era*

- Martin Luther: Luther spoke extensively about the importance of prayer in combating spiritual forces. He famously wrote about standing firm in faith through prayer against the devil's tactics, specifically in the hymn "A Mighty Fortress Is Our God."

- The Use of Scripture in Prayer: During the Reformation, reformers emphasized the power of Scripture in prayer, seeing it as a weapon against darkness.

5. *Modern Instances*

- Prayer Movements: In the 20th and 21st centuries, various prayer movements have emerged, focusing on intercession against different societal issues viewed as demonic influences, like poverty or violence. For example, the 24-7 Prayer Movement encourages continuous prayer as a way to influence spiritual battles globally.

- Deliverance Ministries: Many contemporary churches have prayer ministries dedicated to deliverance, where prayer is integral in invoking divine assistance to free individuals from perceived demonic oppression.

6. *Intercessory Prayer*

- The practice of intercessory prayer, where individuals or groups pray on behalf of others, is prevalent in many religious communities. This is often viewed as a direct confrontation with negative spiritual influences. The concept is rooted in passages like James 5:16, which speaks of the power of prayer to heal.

- During the 2021 pandemic, church members and I would meet at the ministry, lock ourselves inside, and pray for hours, not knowing the time or even worrying about food. Nothing else mattered but being in the presence of God.

> Confess your faults one to another, and pray one for another, that ye may be healed. The effectual fervent prayer of a righteous man availeth much.
>
> — JAMES 5:16

Historically, prayer has been seen as a powerful tool in spiritual warfare. From biblical times through to contemporary practices, believers across various traditions have utilized prayer to seek divine intervention and support in battling not just personal struggles but broader spiritual conflicts. The belief in the potency of prayer against demonic forces continues to inspire individuals and communities to engage in spiritual disciplines aimed at both personal and collective liberation from darkness.

A TESTIMONY OF OBEDIENCE IN PRAYER

I remember back in 2016, I was at home on a seven-day fast, reading my Bible and praying all day. There was a knock on the door, so I went to see who it was. Checking through my window, I saw a friend I had known for years, asking me for help with another friend who was demon-possessed. I didn't go anywhere until the Lord released me and said, "GO." So I replied, "Yes, Sir, I will go," and I grabbed my prayer shawl and my anointing oil and told them, "Let's go to the beach," where the Holy Spirit instructed me to take them.

While traveling on the road to the beach, the Holy Spirit revealed the name of the demon to me, and I called the demon by name. The demon began to choke the lady while she was driving, so she had to park on the side of the road. I heard the demon cursing me through the lady. We waited until the demon calmed down so that our friend could continue driving to the beach. We stopped at a nearby grocery store close to our destination to grab a small bottle of water, then proceeded to the beach.

When we arrived at the beach, we walked away from the area where people were swimming to a quiet spot by the sea. The Holy Spirit instructed me to call upon angels to trouble the water for healing and deliverance, just like in John, chapter 5, where Jesus healed a man who had been sick for 38 years at the Pool of Bethesda. He also instructed me to pray over the water. The significance of praying over the oil and water before use was so that the oil could be used for God's glory, righteousness, and holiness wherever it was applied, even for healing.

The oil may have been used as a physical symbol that someone was being set apart for God's purposes or as part of a sacrament of healing. Anointing oil is a symbol of the Holy Spirit coming to heal, empower, and bless.

 Is any man sick among you? Let him bring in the priests of the church and let them pray over him, anointing him with oil in the name of the Lord. And let the prayer of faith save the sick man.

— JAMES 5:14–15

After anointing the lady, the demon manifested and began cursing me, saying, "Leave her alone. She is mine," referring to the lady. The Holy Spirit said to me, "Command that demon to get out NOW," in a loud, commanding voice. I repeated what He said, and here came deliverance. The lady began vomiting things out of her mouth. Then the Holy Spirit told me, "It is done." Amen.

Being led by the Spirit of God to deliver a soul brings great joy in setting His children free from bondage and removing the yoke of Satan. The woman was set free and delivered.

CHAPTER TWO

PREPARING FOR PRAYER

Before you begin praying the warfare prayers, it is essential to prepare your heart, mind, and spirit. Spiritual warfare is not casual or carnal—it is intentional, holy, and rooted in faith.

POSTURE YOUR HEART

The effectiveness of your prayers is not about how loud you pray or how many words you use, but about the posture of your heart and your alignment with the Spirit of God.

The Word of God reminds us:

> But without faith it is impossible to please Him, for he who comes to God must believe that He is, and that He is a rewarder of those who diligently seek Him.
>
> — HEBREWS 11:6

Every word you speak in prayer must be anchored in faith,

believing that God hears you and will respond according to His will. Faith is your spiritual currency in warfare. When you pray, you're not just speaking into the air—you are activating divine authority. You are standing in agreement with heaven and releasing God's will on earth.

Your intention in prayer also matters. Spiritual warfare is not about vengeance or fear—it's about aligning your spirit with the purposes of God. Come to prayer with a clean heart, a submitted will, and a desire to see God's kingdom prevail in your life and in the lives of others.

Just as the priests in the Old Testament washed before entering the temple, we, too, must spiritually prepare ourselves before stepping into warfare. Here are a few practices to help you cleanse and center yourself before prayer:

- *Repent and Confess:* Ask the Holy Spirit to reveal any sin, bitterness, or unforgiveness in your heart. Confess it before the Lord and receive His cleansing (1 John 1:9).

- *Worship and Thanksgiving:* Enter into God's presence with praise. Worship opens the heavens and softens your heart, allowing you to connect with the Spirit of God.

- *Quiet Your Mind:* Turn off distractions and spend a few minutes in silence or listening to worship music to calm your soul. This helps you focus and become more sensitive to the Holy Spirit's leading.

- *Anoint Yourself:* If you feel led, anoint your head or hands with oil as a symbol of consecration. Declare aloud that you are set apart for God's purposes.

- *Speak Scripture Over Yourself:* Declare passages like Psalm 51:10 (*"Create in me a clean heart, O God"*) or Psalm 24:3-4

("*Who may ascend the mountain of the Lord? He who has clean hands and a pure heart*") to ready your spirit for battle.

When your heart is clean, your focus is clear, and your faith is activated, you are fully prepared to engage in prayer with power and precision. Let this be your sacred moment of alignment with God—before you war, you must worship, and before you decree, you must discern.

Now that your heart is prepared, let us explore the different types of prayers and how to use them strategically in your spiritual warfare journey.

TEN TYPES OF PRAYER

When it comes to spiritual warfare and prayers against demonic forces, various traditions offer distinct forms of prayers. Here are some common types of prayers that people may use for spiritual protection and warfare against demonic influences:

1. *Supplication Prayers*

These are prayers where believers ask for God's help, protection, and strength to overcome demonic forces.

Example:

- "Lord, I ask for Your protection against any evil spirits attempting to come against me. Surround me with Your light and keep me safe."

Fear not, for I am with you; be not dismayed, for I am your God; I will strengthen you, I will help you, I will uphold you with my righteous right hand.

— ISAIAH 41:10

2. *Prayers of Authority*

These prayers affirm the believer's authority over demonic powers through faith in Jesus Christ.

Example:

- "In the name of Jesus, I rebuke any spirit of darkness trying to attack my life. I command you to leave and never return."

3. *Intercessory Prayers*

In these prayers, someone may stand in the gap for others, praying for their deliverance from demonic influence.

Example:

- "Heavenly Father, I intercede for my friend (call their name/names) who is struggling. I pray that You break the chains of darkness holding them captive."

You are my hiding place; you will protect me from trouble and surround me with songs of deliverance.

— PSALM 32:7

4. *Deliverance Prayers*

These are specific prayers asking for deliverance from demonic oppression or possession.

Example:

- "Lord, I seek Your deliverance from this spiritual bondage. Cleanse me and set me free from all evil."

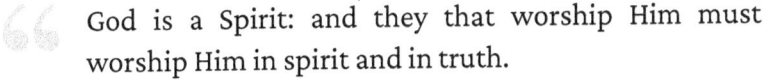 When the righteous cry for help, the LORD hears and delivers them out of all their troubles.

— PSALM 34:17

5. *Prayers of Praise and Worship*

Uplifting God in praise can be a powerful weapon against negativity and darkness.

Example:

- "I praise You, Lord, for Your power and might. Your light drives away all shadows. I worship You and acknowledge Your sovereignty over my life."

God is a Spirit: and they that worship Him must worship Him in spirit and in truth.

— JOHN 4:24

6. *Scripture-Based Prayers*

Using Bible verses to form prayers can be very effective.

Example:

- "I claim Psalm 91, dwelling in the secret place of the Most High and declaring that no evil shall befall me."

The Lord is my shepherd, I lack nothing. He makes me lie down in green pastures; He leads me beside quiet waters. He refreshes my soul.

— PSALM 23:1-5

7. *Cleansing Prayers*

These are prayers asking for spiritual cleansing and purification from any negative influence.

Example:

- "Father, cleanse me from all unrighteousness and remove everything that is not of You from my life."

"Create in me a clean heart, O God, and put a new and right spirit within me."

— PSALM 51:10

8. *Prayers for Strength and Courage*

These are prayers asking for strength to face spiritual battles.

Example:

- "Lord, grant me the courage to stand firm against any evil that comes my way. Fill me with Your strength.

Have I not commanded you? Be strong and of a good courage; be not afraid, neither be thou dismayed: for the Lord thy God is with thee whithersoever thou goest.

— JOSHUA 1:9

9. *Fasting and Prayer*

Combining fasting with prayer is often used as a means to deepen spiritual authority and clarity.

Example:

- "Lord Jesus, as I fast and pray, I seek Your guidance and strength, Lord, to overcome the forces of darkness."

 Jesus told His disciples that prayer and fasting can help deal with difficult situations and build a stronger relationship with God.

— MATTHEW 9:14-15

10. *Community Prayer*

These are group prayers where individuals come together to pray against demonic forces.

Example:

- "Together, we bind every spirit of darkness in this place, declaring the victory of Christ over every stronghold."

Always ensure that prayers are done with faith and conviction, aligning with your belief system. It's also essential to maintain a life of integrity and righteousness, as spiritual warfare is not just about speaking words but living in accordance with the principles of faith.

THREE PILLARS OF WARFARE PRAYER

As you prepare to engage in spiritual warfare, it's important to recognize the three foundational movements that often function together in prayer: *invocation*, *intercession*, and *deliverance*. Each of these carries a distinct purpose, and when used under the guidance of the Holy Spirit, they become powerful tools in destroying the works of darkness.

1. *Invocation*: Calling on divine authority

Invocation is the act of inviting the presence, power, and protection of God into your situation. It is a sacred declaration that you are not fighting in your own strength—you are calling on heaven's army to fight on your behalf.

When you invoke God's name, you are activating divine jurisdiction over a matter. This includes calling on the name of Jesus, invoking the power of the blood, and acknowledging the presence of the Holy Spirit. Invocation sets the atmosphere for warfare and establishes a spiritual covering over you and those you are praying for.

 The name of the Lord is a strong tower; the righteous run to it and are safe.

— PROVERBS 18:10

Use invocation at the beginning of your prayers to declare that God is the One leading the charge, and that every demonic presence must bow to His name.

2. *Intercession*: Standing in the gap for others

Intercession is spiritual advocacy. It is the selfless act of praying on behalf of someone else—especially those who are under attack, bound by darkness, or unable to pray for themselves. Intercessors are spiritual gatekeepers who stand between the forces of hell and the people of God.

True intercession requires compassion, discernment, and persistence. You may find yourself weeping, travailing, or praying in tongues as the Holy Spirit gives utterance. When you intercede, you are partnering with heaven to pull someone out of spiritual danger and into divine protection and restoration.

 I sought for a man among them who would make a wall, and stand in the gap before Me on behalf of the land...

— EZEKIEL 22:30

3. *Deliverance*: Breaking the chains of darkness

Deliverance is the divine removal of demonic influence. These are prayers aimed at casting out spirits, breaking generational curses, and reclaiming territory that the enemy has tried to occupy. Deliverance is a demonstration of the authority given to believers through Jesus Christ.

This type of prayer often involves identifying the root of oppression, renouncing legal rights the enemy may have claimed, and commanding spirits to leave in the name of Jesus. Deliverance must always be grounded in love, compassion, and scriptural truth.

> And these signs will follow those who believe: In My name they will cast out demons...

— MARK 16:17

Deliverance is not just about removing the enemy—it's about restoring wholeness and ushering in the presence of the Holy Spirit where darkness once dwelled.

Each of these expressions of prayer—invocation, intercession, and deliverance—plays a unique and vital role in spiritual warfare. They often overlap, and as you grow in discernment, the Holy Spirit will show you which one is needed in a given moment.

Each of these expressions of prayer—invocation, intercession, and deliverance—plays a unique and vital role in spiritual warfare. While they each serve different functions, they often work together to confront, dismantle, and overcome the forces of darkness.

Before we move into the ministry of intercession, it is crucial to understand the role of angelic assistance in spiritual warfare. God has assigned angels to protect, defend, and minister to His people, especially during times of battle. In the next section, we will explore how to call upon divine angels for protection and how to position yourself to receive supernatural help from heaven's army.

Let us now step into this powerful dimension of angelic protection, where God's messengers are released to war on your behalf.

INVOCATION: CALLING ON GOD'S ARMY

Calling upon divine angels for protection can be a personal and spiritual practice. Here are some steps you might consider:

1. *Set Your Intention*: Begin by clearly defining your intention. This could be a prayer or a simple request for protection.

2. *Create a Sacred Space:* Find a quiet place where you can focus and feel safe. You might want to go deep into worship by playing songs to enhance the atmosphere.

3. *Meditation and Prayer:* Enter a state of meditation or prayer. You can speak directly to the angels, asking for their protection. Some people find it helpful to use specific prayers or invocations.

4. *Visualize the Protection:* Imagine a protective light surrounding you. Visualizing this can help you feel more connected to the energy of the angels.

5. *Ask for Specific Angels:* You can call upon specific angels known for protection, such as Archangel Michael and Warring Angels, often considered protectors against negative energies and harm.

6. *Express Gratitude:* Thank the God for His presence and for allowing the protection of His angels.

7. *Trust the Process:* Finally, trust that the angels are responding to your call. Be open to God's guidance and support in any form it may come.

Your specific practices may vary, so feel free to adapt these suggestions to what resonates most with you.

INTERCESSION: PRAYING FOR OTHERS

Intercession is the spirutual act of standing in the gap for others, lifting them up in prayer when they cannot fight for themselves. You should intercede with compassion, precision, and biblical authority to bring breakthrough and protection to those under spiritual attack. Here is some additional wisdom you might consider when interceding on behalf of others:

- *Understanding:* Begin by understanding the situation of those you wish to pray for. This may involve listening to their experiences and showing empathy, as well as seeking guidance from the Holy Spirit on how to approach the situation.

- *Example Prayer of Intercession:* You might pray something like: "Heavenly Father, I come before You, asking for Your protection over [Name]. Shield them from any negative influences and surround them with Your love and light. May Your peace cover them and restore their spirit."

- *Scriptural References:* Incorporate relevant scriptures, such as Psalm 91:1 and Ephesians 6:11-12.

He who dwells in the secret place of the Most High shall abide under the shadow of the Almighty.

— PSALM 91:1

 Put on the full armor of God, so that you can take your stand against the devil's schemes.

— EPHESIANS 6:11-12

DELIVERANCE: SPECIFIC PRAYERS TO EXPEL DEMONS

Deliverance prayer is a powerful and intentional act of confronting and expelling demonic forces through the authority of Jesus Christ. Consider the following wisdom to break spiritual bondage and claim victory:

1. *Preparation*: Ensure the environment is calm and conducive to prayer. You may choose to start by repenting and playing worship music. Many services begin with worship, inviting the presence of the Spirit of the living God, during which demons may manifest.

2. *Example Prayer for Deliverance*: Use direct and specific language. A prayer might look like: "In the name of Jesus, I take full authority, power, and dominion over every spirit that is not of God. I command any unclean spirit or demonic presence affecting [Name] to leave now. I release the fire of God against you. You have no authority here. I serve you an eviction notice now in the name of Jesus. Out of this vessel right now in the mighty name of Jesus, and never return. I declare freedom, healing, and restoration over them in Jesus' name."

3. *Scriptural Refernces*: Reinforce your prayers with scripture, such as Luke 10:19 and Mark 16:17.

> Behold, I have given you authority to trample on serpents and scorpions, and over all the power of the enemy, and nothing shall hurt you.
>
> — LUKE 10:19

> And these signs will accompany those who believe: in my name they will cast out demons...
>
> — MARK 16:17

SUPPORT THAT SUSTAINS

Spiritual warfare doesn't end at deliverance—it often marks the beginning of a renewed journey of faith, healing, and discipleship. After someone experiences breakthrough, they will need continual support, guidance, and accountability to remain free and spiritually grounded. Deliverance is not a one-time event; it is a lifestyle of walking in truth, obedience, and fellowship with the Holy Spirit.

Just as Jesus instructed the healed to "go and sin no more," it is important to lovingly walk alongside those who've received deliverance to help them remain free. Without proper discipleship and spiritual discipline, individuals may unknowingly return to behaviors or environments that open doors to demonic re-entry. Scripture warns in Luke 11:26 that if a person is not filled with the Spirit and guarded after deliverance, the enemy may return with seven more spirits, leaving the person worse off than before.

Provide regular check-ins. These can be as simple as a phone call, prayer meeting, or devotional study together. Encourage them to stay in the Word, surround themselves with a faith-filled community, and continue spiritual disciplines such as prayer, fasting, journaling, and worship. Be a source of accountability as well as compassion.

Recognize that spiritual maturity takes time. Support them through relapses or questions without judgment—your presence alone can be a lifeline. Always approach these situations with humility, discernment, and love, pointing them continually back to Jesus Christ, who is their true Deliverer and Sustainer.

Also, remember that every person's faith journey looks different. While the tools and prayers in this book are powerful, be led by the Holy Spirit in how you support each individual, honoring their pace and God's timing in their transformation.

PART TWO
EXPOSING DARKNESS

The Bible tells us in Ephesians 5:11, "Have nothing to do with the fruitless deeds of darkness, but rather expose them." As believers, we are called not only to reject the works of the enemy but also to understand how they operate so that we can effectively engage in spiritual warfare.

So, as we continue on this journey, it's important to equip ourselves with a deeper knowledge of the enemy's tactics. Spiritual warfare isn't just reactive—it's strategic. In the next section, we will begin exposing the hidden works of darkness that often go unnoticed or unaddressed in the lives of believers. By shedding light on these deceptive strategies, we can be fully equipped with biblical wisdom, prayer, and the power of the Holy Spirit to overcome them. Each teaching will be followed by specific prayers for deliverance and protection— tailored to dismantle strongholds, resist demonic attacks, and walk in authority.

So, get ready to shine light into dark places. What you will discover next will not only protect you, but empower you to stand firm in Christ's victory and set others free.

CHAPTER FOUR
UNDERSTANDING UNDERGROUND DEMONS

Demons are often described as supernatural beings that embody evil or malevolence in various religious, mythological, and folklore traditions. They are typically perceived as entities capable of influencing or possessing humans, leading them to sin or harm. The characteristics and roles of demons vary significantly across cultures and religions:

1. Religious Perspectives:

- Christianity: Demons are often viewed as fallen angels or spirits opposed to God and His angels. They are believed to tempt, deceive, and possess individuals, causing illness or moral corruption. The Bible describes various types of demons and their activities.

- Islam: In Islam, demons are referred to as "jinn." Created from smokeless fire, jinn can be good, evil, or neutral.

Shaitan (or Shaytan) is associated with evil jinn who lead humans astray.

- Hinduism and Buddhism: These traditions have their own concepts of malevolent spirits or beings, such as asuras in Hinduism and Mara in Buddhism, who oppose the divine or create obstacles to enlightenment.

2. Folklore and Mythology:

- Many cultures have stories of demons or evil spirits that are thought to inhabit certain places, manipulate humans, or bring disaster. These figures often serve as cautionary tales or as explanations for natural phenomena or human behavior.

3. Psychological Interpretations:

- In modern times, demons are often viewed metaphorically, representing internal struggles, fears, or societal issues. Some psychological frameworks interpret "demons" as aspects of the human psyche that manifest in negative behaviors or thoughts.

4. Pop Culture:

- The portrayal of demons has permeated literature, film, and art, often emphasizing horror elements. These depictions range from traditional religious representations to more creative and imaginative interpretations in the horror genre.

Overall, demons have been a significant part of human culture for centuries, serving various roles depending on the context in which they appear.

TYPES OF UNDERGROUND DEMONS

The concept of an "underground world" appears in many cultures and mythologies, often associated with spiritual implications, the afterlife, and various supernatural beings such as demons or spirits. Below is an overview of common themes surrounding the underground realm and its spiritual significance:

1. Afterlife and the Underworld:

- Many cultures view the underground realm as a place of the dead or a transitional area to the afterlife. For instance, in ancient Egyptian beliefs, the underworld (Duat) was where souls journeyed after death, facing judgment before moving on.

- In Christianity, Hell is often depicted as an underground realm where demons and lost souls reside, emphasizing the moral consequences of earthly actions.

2. Personal Transformation:

- The underground often symbolizes a journey into the subconscious or a process of personal transformation. It represents delving deeper within oneself to confront fears or unresolved issues, ultimately leading to spiritual growth.

3. Fertility and Renewal:

- Many cultures associate the underground with fertility due to its connection with the earth. The idea of seeds planted in the ground, which later sprout, reflects regeneration and the cyclical nature of life and death.

4. Hidden Knowledge and Mysteries:

- The underground realm is often viewed as a repository of hidden knowledge and mysteries. This may include ancient wisdom, chthonic deities, or secrets that are not immediately accessible to the average person.

MYTHS AND BELIEFS ABOUT UNDERGROUND DEMONS

Below are four myths surrounding the beliefs that are withheld regarding the underground world of demonic spirits.

1. Chthonic Deities:

- Many mythologies feature gods and spirits associated with the underground. In Greek mythology, Hades is the ruler of the Underworld. These deities often have dual characteristics, embodying both fertility (as they are associated with the earth) and death.

2. Demons and Spirits:

- Various cultures have beliefs in demons that dwell underground. These beings are often depicted as malevolent and are associated with darkness, chaos, and fear. In folktales, these demons may lure individuals into the depths, signifying temptation and moral decay.

3. Protection Against the Underground:

- Rituals and protective measures are common in folklore to guard against negative underground entities. This may include offerings to spirits or deities, as well as the use of charms or amulets to provide protection from harm.

4. Symbolic Representations:

- Underground demons can symbolize human fears and anxieties. They often represent the darker aspects of human nature or societal fears, such as death, the unknown, or the consequences of sin.

CHAPTER FIVE
THE DEMONIC REALM

Understanding demonic forces involves exploring various cultural, religious, psychological, and philosophical frameworks. Below are some key points to consider:

1. Cultural Perspectives:

- Mythology and Folklore: Many cultures have myths that personify evil as demonic beings. These stories often serve to explain moral concepts, human fears, or the nature of good and evil.

- Religious Views: In Christianity, demons are generally understood as fallen angels or spirits opposed to God, often associated with sin and temptation. In other religions, such as Hinduism and Buddhism, malevolent forces are interpreted differently, reflecting unique spiritual and cultural beliefs.

2. Psychological Aspects:

- Projection of Internal Conflict: Some psychologists suggest that what people interpret as demonic forces may actually be manifestations of internal struggles, fears, or unresolved traumas.

- Symbolic Representation: Demons can also symbolize human vices or failings, representing aspects of the psyche that individuals find threatening or difficult to confront.

3. Demonology:

- Study of Demons: Demonology is an academic and theological field that examines the nature of demons, their characteristics, and their perceived impact on human lives.

- Rituals and Exorcisms: Across various traditions, rituals and prayers are used to banish or control demonic forces, often through practices like exorcisms or spiritual cleansings.

4. Literature and Media:

- Popular Culture: Demons frequently appear in literature, films, and video games, shaping public perceptions of these forces and often reflecting societal fears or anxieties.

- Symbolism in Art: Artists have historically depicted demons to explore themes such as evil, temptation, and the eternal struggle between good and evil.

5. Philosophical Considerations

- The Nature of Evil: Philosophical questions often arise about the nature of evil, including whether demonic forces are external entities or inherent aspects of human nature.

- Free Will and Morality: Discussions about demons often lead to considerations of free will, the nature of sin, and the question of moral responsibility.

Understanding demonic forces is a complex endeavor, as it intertwines with various disciplines, including theology, psychology, cultural studies, and the arts. Exploring these perspectives can offer deeper insights into the human condition and our understanding of good and evil.

DEMONIC RITUALS AND PRACTICES

Rituals and practices in what is often referred to as the "demonic world" can vary widely depending on cultural, religious, and individual beliefs. Here are some common elements that might be associated with such rituals:

1. Invocation and Summoning

- Purpose: Practitioners may seek to summon or invoke demons or other supernatural entities for guidance, power, or specific favors.

- Methods: This often involves specific prayers, chants, or symbols, and can take place in a ritual setting with altars and offerings.

2. Offerings and Sacrifices

- Types of Offerings: Offerings can include food, incense, symbols, or in some darker practices, blood from animal or human sacrifices.

- Intent: The goal is generally to appease the entity, gain favor, or ask for assistance in a particular matter.

3. Divination and Scrying

- Purpose: Used to gain insight or knowledge from demons or to foresee future events.

- Methods: Practices like using crystal balls, tarot cards, or other divination tools can be involved.

4. Ritual Magic

- Types: This can include both ceremonial magic and folk magic, using various spells aimed at manipulating supernatural forces.

- Function: People may perform rituals to achieve specific goals (e.g., love, financial success, protection from enemies).

5. Curses and Hexes

- Purpose: Some practitioners may perform rituals intended to harm others or to seek revenge.

- Ethics: The morality of such practices is often debated and viewed negatively in many cultures.

6. Cleansing and Protection Rituals

- Methods: These rituals are done to cleanse oneself of negative energies or to protect against perceived demonic influences.

- Tools: Common tools can include salt, herbs, and protective symbols.

7. Rituals of Dedication

- Purpose: Some individuals may practice rituals to dedicate themselves to a particular demon or entity as part of a spiritual path.

- Dedication: This often involves oaths, promises, or offerings to signify commitment.

8. Altar Construction

- Purpose: An altar may be set up as a sacred space for rituals, housing symbols, offerings, and other items related to the practice.

- Design: Altars are often personalized and can vary in complexity.

It's important to note that beliefs around these rituals vary enormously between different cultures and religious practices. What one group considers a form of demonic worship, another might view as benign. Many of these practices are shrouded in superstition and folklore, so they should be approached with sensitivity and understanding of the context in which they arise.

CHAPTER SIX
SPIRITUAL WARFARE INSIGHTS

To effectively engage in spiritual warfare, Believers must not only pray but also discern the strategies of the enemy. The kingdom of darkness is highly calculated, using specific times, objects, and rituals to release curses, manipulation, and bondage into the earth.

This chapter exposes some of the tools and timings that witches and warlocks use to carry out their assignments. By the leading of the Holy Spirit, this knowledge is shared not to glorify darkness, but to equip you to pray with precision, dismantle hidden operations, and take back spiritual territory with boldness and understanding.

TIMES OF RITUALS

Witches and warlocks often perform rituals during specific times, including 12 noon, 12 midnight, 3 a.m., and 6 a.m. As an intercessor, prayer warrior, or gatekeeper, these are crucial prayer watch times that you should pay attention to.

PURE SACRIFICES

Pure sacrifices, such as an infant or someone who is a virgin, are often used by witches and warlocks to gain power. These sacrifices are typically performed to obtain wealth, cause the death of a family member, inflict harm on someone, or bring sickness that leads to death.

SHAMBALLA BEADS

Witches and warlocks use Shamballa beads to invoke spirits and cast spells. They call upon demons to perform tasks for them, such as providing protection or manipulating unseen forces to shield them from harm.

CRESINS

Cresins are tools used by witches and warlocks in conjunction with dolls or photographs. Items such as pins, threads, needles, and cords are used to harm individuals. These tools are employed to afflict the human body, causing inflammation and other physical ailments. This practice is referred to as bondage. The Holy Spirit has revealed this to teach His people how to engage in spiritual warfare.

CANDLES

Witches and warlocks use candles of various colors to summon spirits from the spiritual realm. These rituals are often performed to bring good luck, prosperity, or control over another person's mind. While burning candles, they summon spirits for purposes such as separation, love manipulation, sickness, hindrance from achieving goals, and more.

CARBON PAPER

Witches and warlocks also use carbon paper in their rituals. They write down a person's information (such as their name, date of birth, and other details) on the paper and chant over it while placing a candle on top. The carbon paper is believed to serve as a medium for channeling their intentions, which may include predictions or curses directed at the individual.

* * *

I pray that the instructions laid on my heart by the Holy Spirit will help you stay vigilant and alert when dealing with cultural demons and spirits from around the world. These insights are shared to make you aware of the kinds of spirits and demonic forces you may encounter.

Ephesians 6:12 reminds us:

> For we wrestle not against flesh and blood, but against principalities, against powers, against the rulers of the darkness of this world, against spiritual wickedness in high places.

> — EPHESIANS 6:12

As you continue throughout this book, you will learn more about the differences in demonic forces and how they operate. Please note that much of my study on demonology and folklore has been supported by research through the internet, including pictures and dictionary references.

PART THREE
ELEMENTS OF
WITCHCRAFT

This section unveils the tangible tools and tactics often used in witchcraft and occult rituals to manipulate, curse, or bind others through demonic influence. From voodoo dolls and blood sacrifices to amulets, graveyard dirt, and stolen personal items, each chapter explores how these objects are used as entry points for spiritual attack. With biblical insight and strategic prayers, this section will equip you to recognize these dark elements, break their power, and reclaim your spiritual territory through the authority of Jesus Christ.

CHAPTER SEVEN
VOODOO DOLLS

Voodoo dolls are often used by witches, warlocks, and practitioners of various forms of magic as tools of influence, intention-setting, and spell work. Though commonly associated with Voodoo, an Afro-Caribbean religion, similar practices can be found in folk magic traditions across different cultures.

Why Voodoo Dolls Are Used

1. *Symbolic Representation*: A voodoo doll often represents a person whom the practitioner wishes to influence. The doll serves as a physical conduit for their energy, intentions, or spells.
2. *Spiritual Connection:* Practitioners may use a doll to create a spiritual link to their target. Through various rituals, they believe they can manipulate circumstances in the target's life.

While some may use these dolls for what they perceive as "positive" purposes, in the spiritual realm, any form of witchcraft invites demonic influence. The Word of God warns against all forms of sorcery and calls believers to rely solely on Him for guidance and power (Deuteronomy 18:10-12).

DELIVERANCE FROM VOODOO & SPIRITUAL MANIPULATION

The power of Jesus Christ is greater than any work of darkness. Deliverance from spiritual oppression caused by voodoo or similar practices comes through prayer, faith in God, and the authority of Scripture.

5 Steps to Spiritual Freedom

1. *Prayer:* Seek God's protection and renounce any spiritual ties to witchcraft.
2. *Scripture Reading:* Stand on God's promises, such as Psalm 91, which declares His protection.
3. *Faith and Affirmation:* Declare your freedom in Christ and reject fear.
4. *Community Support:* Seek prayer support from your church or spiritual leaders.
5. *Reject Fear:* Fear gives the enemy a foothold. Trust in God's power and stand firm in faith.

PRAYERS FOR DELIVERANCE FROM VOODOO DOLLS

Heavenly Father, I come before You and ask for Your divine protection. According to Psalm 91:1-2, I dwell in the secret place of the Most High and abide under the shadow of the Almighty. I declare that You are my refuge and my fortress, my God, in whom I trust. Protect me from all forms of evil and harm, including any witchcraft or voodoo practices. In Jesus' mighty name, Amen.

Lord Jesus, I seek Your deliverance from any curse or bondage that has come upon me through voodoo practices. Your Word says in Luke 4:18 that You came to proclaim freedom for the prisoners. I claim that freedom now and break any chains that bind me. I declare that I am free in You, Lord Jesus.

In the Name of Jesus, I break every curse and hex that has been placed upon me. According to Galatians 3:13, Christ has redeemed me from the curse of the law by becoming a curse for me. I renounce every voodoo influence and proclaim my liberty in Christ.

Father, I thank You for Your promise of restoration. In Joel 2:25, You promise to restore the years that the locust has eaten. I ask that You restore everything that has been taken from me by any witchcraft or voodoo-related practices. Bring healing to every area of my life affected by these influences.

Mighty God, I ask for Your divine intervention against any attacks from the enemy. As stated in Isaiah 54:17, no weapon formed against me shall prosper. I stand firm on this promise and declare that every voodoo doll and its influence over my life is rendered powerless and ineffective. I trust in Your authority, Lord. Amen.

CHAPTER EIGHT
AMULETS

Amulets are often used as protective or magical tools in various forms of witchcraft. While some may view them as mere cultural symbols, many are crafted with the intent of invoking spiritual power—often unknowingly inviting demonic influence.

Regardless of their intended purpose, amulets open spiritual doors that can lead to demonic oppression. As believers, we place our trust in God alone—not in objects, charms, or talismans (Exodus 20:3-5).

Witches and warlocks often use amulets as protective or magical tools. Here are a few reasons why they might use them on people:

1. *Protection:* Amulets are commonly believed to offer protection against negative energies, spirits, or curses. Wearing an amulet can help individuals feel safer and shielded from harm.
2. *Healing:* Some amulets are thought to have healing properties and can be used to promote physical or emotional wellness.

3. *Attraction of Positive Energies:* Amulets can be used to attract love, wealth, or success. They are often charged with specific intentions to enhance those aspects in the wearer's life.

4. *Spiritual Connection:* Certain amulets may be used to strengthen spiritual connections, such as enhancing intuition or connecting with deities and ancestors.

5. *Ritual Use:* In many magical practices, amulets play a role in rituals. They can be used to focus energy and intention during spells or ceremonies.

The specific beliefs and uses can vary widely among different traditions and practitioners in the realm of witchcraft and magic. How can a person be free from witches and warlocks having them bind up in bondage from an amulet?

Finding freedom from the influence of witches, warlocks, or any form of spiritual oppression through God's word involves several steps rooted in faith, prayer, and scripture. Here are some suggestions:

1. *Prayer for Protection:* Begin with prayer, asking God to protect you and to help you renounce any negative influences. Psalms 91 is a powerful chapter to reflect on, as it speaks of God's protection.

2. *Study the Scriptures:* Engage deeply with the Bible. Verses such as Isaiah 54:17 ("No weapon forged against you will prevail") and Ephesians 6:10-18 (the Armor of God) can offer strength. Regular reading can help reinforce your faith.

3. *Faith in God's Power:* Trust in God's power over any dark forces. James 4:7 encourages believers to "Submit yourselves, then, to God. Resist the devil, and he will flee from you."

4. *Renounce Evil:* Verbally renounce any ties to witchcraft, fear, or reliance on amulets or charms. Acknowledge that your protection comes from God alone.
5. *Seek Fellowship:* Connect with a supportive community, such as a church or a prayer group. Having a group to pray with can strengthen your resolve and provide encouragement.
6. *Use the Name of Jesus:* In spiritual warfare, the name of Jesus is powerful. Confidently invoke His name in your prayers for protection and deliverance.
7. *Live in Faith:* Cultivate a strong, faithful life through worship, understanding God's promises, and living out the teachings of Jesus. This strengthens your spiritual defenses.
8. *Consult Spiritual Leaders:* If feeling overwhelmed, it may be helpful to seek guidance from an experienced pastor or spiritual leader who can provide support and prayer.

Remember, spiritual freedom is a journey and can take time. Consistency in faith and reliance on God's word is key.

PRAYERS FOR DELIVERANCE FROM AMULETS

Heavenly Father, I come to You in the name of Jesus Christ. I declare that no weapon formed against me shall prosper. I cover myself and my loved ones with the blood of Jesus. I ask that You break every chain of bondage linked to any amulets or harmful objects.

In the mighty name of Jesus, I renounce and reject every covenant made with amulets, charms, or any form of idolatry. I pull down every stronghold that has been established against my life and declare freedom and deliverance. Lord, let Your fire consume every evil association.

I command every spirit associated with amulets to leave my life and my family right now in the name of Jesus. I declare that I am a child of God, covered by His power and authority. Every spirit of fear, confusion, and darkness is bound and cast out NOW.

In the Name of Jesus, I take authority over every spiritual entity connected to any amulet or charm. I declare they have no power over me, for I am washed by the blood of the Lamb. I claim my deliverance and restoration today.

O Lord, I thank You for the victory You have given me through Jesus Christ. I declare that I am free from the influence of any amulet. I stand firm in the truth of Your Word, which says that Whom the Son sets free is free indeed (John 8:36). Amen.

CHAPTER NINE
BLOOD SACRIFICE

B lood sacrifice is a practice historically associated with various cultures and belief systems, often involving the offering of blood to deities or spirits during rituals. In the context of witches and warlocks, interpretations and practices can vary widely:

1. *Symbolic Offerings:* In many modern neopagan practices, blood sacrifice is often symbolic rather than literal. It may involve the use of red wine or fruit juices to represent blood.

2. *Ritualistic Practices:* Some belief systems include rituals where a small amount of an individual's own blood is used in ceremonies. This is typically done to connect with spiritual forces, seek protection, or invoke spells. Such practices are usually carried out with great care to ensure safety and are not intended to harm others or animals.

3. *Animal Sacrifices:* Historically, certain cultures and traditions practiced animal sacrifices, believing these offerings would appease spirits or gods. However, many

modern practitioners reject this practice in favor of more ethical and symbolic alternatives.

4. *Personal Growth or Connection:* For some, the act of drawing blood may be viewed as a way to create a deeper personal connection to their practice, symbolizing commitment or the seriousness of their intentions.

It is important to note that the vast majority of individuals identifying as witches or practitioners of Wicca do not engage in blood sacrifice. Instead, they promote harm-free practices that emphasize respect, love, and a connection to the natural world.

HOW TO BE DELIVERED FROM BLOOD SACRIFICE

Seeking deliverance from any form of spiritual oppression, including perceived threats from witchcraft or blood sacrifices, is often grounded in faith and prayer. Here are some suggested steps that individuals may consider, depending on their beliefs:

1. *Prayer and Faith:* Engage in sincere and earnest prayer, asking for God's protection and guidance. Many believe that faith can serve as a shield against spiritual attacks.
2. *Seek Spiritual Guidance:* Reach out to a trusted spiritual leader or pastor. They can offer counsel, support, and, if needed, conduct prayer or deliverance services.
3. *Bible Reading and Study:* Draw strength and wisdom from scripture. Passages about God's protection and deliverance can provide comfort and encouragement.
4. *Fasting:* Some individuals practice fasting as a way to deepen their prayers and seek greater spiritual clarity and strength.
5. *Worship and Fellowship:* Participating in worship and fellowship with others can uplift your spirit and reinforce your faith through the support of a community.

6. *Confession and Repentance:* Reflect on your life for any unconfessed sins and seek forgiveness. Many believe that repentance can create a path for God's deliverance.

7. *Spiritual Warfare:* Educate yourself about spiritual warfare as described in religious texts. This may include specific prayers, declarations, or rituals designed to strengthen your spirit against negativity.

8. *Avoidance of Occult Practices:* Refrain from engaging in practices associated with witchcraft or the occult, as these are often viewed as contrary to faith and may lead to further spiritual distress.

9. *Professional Help:* If feelings of fear or oppression persist, consider seeking assistance from mental health professionals who are familiar with spiritual or religious concerns.

PRAYER AGAINST BLOOD SACRIFICE

Heavenly Father, we come before You in reverence and gratitude for the gift of Your Son, Jesus Christ, who shed His blood for our sins, bringing us into a new covenant of grace and mercy. As we reflect on Your Word, we are reminded of the truth in Leviticus 17:11 —that the life of the flesh is in the blood, and it is through that blood that atonement is made for our souls. We acknowledge that our redemption does not come through the blood of animals or sacrifices, but through the ultimate sacrifice of Your Son, as stated in 1 John 4:10: "In this is love, not that we have loved God but that He loved us and sent His Son to be the propitiation for our sins."

Lord, we stand firmly against any practices that seek to harm or sacrifice life in any form, recognizing that the blood of Jesus is sufficient for our salvation. As we reflect on the significance of His body broken for us, as declared in 1 Corinthians 11:24-30, we are called to examine ourselves and to partake in reverence and holiness—not in the spirit of sacrifice, but in remembrance of His love and grace.

Help us, Father, to honor the sanctity of life, rejecting all forms of blood sacrifice that do not align with the love You have shown us. May we be vessels of Your peace and truth, proclaiming the redemptive power of Jesus' blood in our lives and in the world around us.

In Jesus precious Name, we pray, Amen.

CHAPTER TEN
OBJECTS & PERSONAL BELONGINGS

W itches and warlocks often use clothing, personal belongings, or documents in their practices due to the concept of sympathetic magic, which is based on the principle that objects can hold a connection to individuals or places. Here are a few reasons why these items are used:

1. *Personal Connection*: Items that belong to a person (such as clothing, hair, or other personal effects) are believed to carry a unique connection to that individual. This connection can be utilized in spells or rituals to influence or affect the person's life in some way.

2. *Empowerment of Rituals*: Personal belongings are thought to enhance the power and focus of magical workings. Using an item that has belonged to someone can increase the effectiveness of spells directed at that individual.

3. *Symbolism*: Different items can represent various energies or attributes. For instance, clothing might symbolize identity, while documents may represent agreements, contracts, or intentions.

4. *Manifesting Intentions*: Incorporating specific objects into rituals allows practitioners to better visualize their intentions. The use of tangible items can help focus the mind and solidify the purpose of the spell.
5. *Protection:* In some traditions, personal items are used in protective magic to shield an individual from harm or negative influences.

Overall, the use of personal items in witchcraft and magical rituals is deeply rooted in the belief in interconnectedness and the power of intention.

PRAYER TO DESTROY DEMONIC CONNECTIONS

These prayers focus on breaking connections to clothing, documents, places, and things used by witches and warlocks.

> *Heavenly Father, I come before You in humility, seeking Your protection and guidance. I ask for Your marvelous light to shine upon me and shield me from any darkness. I place my trust in You, my refuge and fortress. (Read Psalm 59.)*
>
> *Lord, I ask that You surround me with Your holy angels and cover me with Your divine protection. Just as David sought refuge from those who sought to harm him, I seek Your grace to guard me against any evil intentions or malice, particularly from those who may attempt to harm me through witchcraft or other dark practices.*
>
> *By the grace of God, I release any negative energy and declare the binding of all malice around me. I ask for Your protection and freedom from all curses cast upon me.*
>
> *I renounce any curses or negative energies directed toward*

me. I place my trust in You, Lord, who are my protector and savior. May Your love and power shield me from all harm.

Thank You, Lord, for hearing my prayer. I trust in Your power to protect me from all evil. May Your light drive out every spirit of darkness, and may I walk in peace and safety. Amen.

CHAPTER ELEVEN
GRAVEYARD DIRT

Witches and warlocks are often associated with the use of graveyard dirt in their practices. This is rooted in folklore, traditional magic, and symbolism. Below are some of the common beliefs surrounding its use:

1. *Connection to Ancestors:* Graveyard dirt is believed to create a connection between practitioners and their ancestors or those who have passed on. It is often used in rituals to honor or summon ancestral spirits.

2. *Protection and Power:* In some traditions, graveyard dirt is thought to provide protection or enhance the effectiveness of spells. It is commonly associated with protective magic and workings related to death and the afterlife.

3. *Spirit Communication:* Graveyard dirt is often seen as a medium for communicating with spirits or the dead. Practitioners may use it in rituals to seek wisdom, guidance, or

assistance from those who have transitioned to the spiritual realm.

4. Symbolism of Death and Transformation: Graveyard dirt symbolizes the cycle of life and death, transformation, and the unseen. It serves as a reminder of mortality and the transient nature of human existence.

5. Curses and Hexes: In darker forms of witchcraft, graveyard dirt is sometimes used in curses or hexes. The belief is that the energy associated with death and decay can be harnessed for harmful or malicious purposes.

6. Elemental Associations: Graveyard dirt is often connected to the Earth element in magical traditions. It is believed to add grounding, stability, and a connection to the physical world in spells and rituals.

PRAYERS AGAINST GRAVEYARD DIRT IN YOUR HOME

> *Heavenly Father, I come before You in the name of Jesus Christ, asking for Your divine protection and cleansing over my home and family.*
>
> *Lord, I renounce and cancel any use of graveyard dirt or any objects connected to it that may have been used against me, my family, or my household. I declare that any curses, hexes, or harmful intentions tied to graveyard dirt are nullified and rendered powerless by the blood of Jesus.*
>
> *I plead the blood of Jesus over every corner of my home, my property, and my loved ones. I ask that You send Your holy angels to guard and protect us from all spiritual attacks.*

In the name of Jesus, I take authority over every spirit of death, decay, and destruction that may have been invoked through graveyard dirt. I bind and cast them out, commanding them to leave my home and never return.

Father, fill my home with Your presence, peace, and light. Let no weapon formed against us prosper (Isaiah 54:17). Thank You, Lord, for Your protection and deliverance. I give You all the glory, honor, and praise. In Jesus' name, I pray. Amen.

Lord Jesus, I come before You, seeking Your divine protection over my home. I ask that You surround my dwelling with Your warring angels, and I call forth Archangel Michael to fight on my behalf. I declare that no weapon formed against me shall prosper (Isaiah 54:17). I ask You to cleanse my home of any negativity and remove any evil influences that may have been brought near. In Jesus' name, I pray.

I pray for the fire and power of God to cover my home. As it is written in Psalm 51:10, *"Create in me a clean heart, O God, and renew a right spirit within me."* I ask that You create a clean and holy space in my home and remove anything that does not align with Your will. Let Your presence fill every corner, driving out all darkness. In Jesus' name, I pray.

The Lord is my light and my salvation; whom shall I fear? * (Psalm 27:1).

I declare that my faith in God shields my home and family from all harm. I plead the blood of Jesus over my property and my loved ones. We are covered and protected

*from all evil. I claim victory over any attempts to
bring darkness into our lives.*

*I ask for Your deliverance from any curses, sorcery, or
witchcraft aimed against me, my family, or my home.
Your Word tells us in Luke 10:19 that we have been
given authority to trample on serpents and scorpions
and to overcome all the power of the enemy; nothing
will harm us. I stand upon this promise and declare
freedom and safety in my household.*

*Thank You, Lord, for Your love and protection. I trust in
Your power to safeguard my home and everyone
within it. May my heart and home be filled with Your
glory and presence, now and forever. I believe and
know without a shadow of a doubt that You are my
refuge and fortress (Psalm 91:2).*

In Jesus' name, I pray. Amen.

PART FOUR
TYPES OF
DEMONIC ENTITIES

This section offers a deeper understanding of the specific spirits believers may encounter in spiritual warfare. From cultural forms of witchcraft such as Haitian, Spanish, and African traditions, to modern demonic spirits like Jezebel, Mara, marine spirits, sexual spirits, and Alamy spirits, each chapter shines a light on the tactics and assignments of these entities.

With scriptural insight and practical prayer strategies, this section equips you to recognize, confront, and overcome the hidden influences of darkness operating across regions, cultures, and generations. Knowledge is power—and in spiritual warfare, discernment is key.

CHAPTER TWELVE
MODERN DEMONIC SPIRITS

In every generation, the enemy rebrands old spirits with new names, adapting to the culture of the times. The 20th and 21st centuries have seen a rise in pop culture depictions of spiritual entities that mirror biblical demonic characteristics—spirits that influence the mind, twist truth, glorify death, and normalize fear. These spirits often masquerade behind entertainment, folklore, social trends, or even misunderstood mental states. As believers, it's important to discern their presence and take authority over them through prayer.

1. The Grim Reaper – Spirit of Death and Fatalism

The Grim Reaper, cloaked in shadows and carrying a sickle, represents more than just the end of physical life—it symbolizes hopelessness, premature death, and the demonic assignment to steal, kill, and destroy (John 10:10). This spirit often lingers around those struggling with chronic illness, suicidal thoughts, or generational curses of death.

> *"Lord, I come against every spirit of premature death and*
> *fear in the name of Jesus. I reject the assignment of the*
> *enemy to bring death before my time. I declare that I*
> *shall live and not die, and declare the works of the*
> *Lord (Psalm 118:17). I plead the blood of Jesus over my*
> *life and break every covenant with fear and death.*
> *Amen."*

2. The Joker – Spirit of Chaos and Insanity

Inspired by media portrayals of villainous clowns or anarchist icons, this spirit thrives in confusion, mockery, and mental torment. The "Joker spirit" fuels self-destruction, nihilism, and violence masked behind humor or rebellion. It often attaches to those struggling with mental instability, unresolved trauma, or addiction.

> *"Father, I renounce every spirit of chaos, confusion, and*
> *mockery that seeks to distract or deceive. I reject*
> *mental torment and disorder. I declare that You are*
> *not the author of confusion but of peace (1*
> *Corinthians 14:33). Restore clarity to my mind and*
> *order to my life, in Jesus' name. Amen."*

3. Slender Man – Spirit of Intimidation and Seduction

This faceless figure represents hidden evil and often seduces through mystery and fear. The Slender Man spirit draws people into darkness subtly—especially youth—through games, curiosity, or supernatural obsession. It partners with intimidation, fear, and spiritual paralysis.

> *"Lord, I expose every hidden spirit of intimidation and*
> *seduction operating in darkness. In Jesus' name, I cast*
> *out every unclean spirit seeking to lure me or my*

family. I break the power of fear and demonic obses-
sion. The light of Christ exposes every dark work
(Ephesians 5:11), and I walk in His authority and
peace. Amen."

4. Bloody Mary – Spirit of Terror and Mirrors of Deception

This spirit is rooted in occult rituals involving mirrors and blood, symbolizing vanity, fear, and demonic summoning. The Bloody Mary spirit opens the door to trauma, fear-based fascination, and the use of reflective tools for divination.

> *"Father God, I renounce every open door through fear,*
> *superstition, or occult games. I shut down every*
> *demonic portal opened through mirrors, blood rituals,*
> *or word curses. I declare that no weapon formed*
> *against me shall prosper (Isaiah 54:17). I plead the*
> *blood of Jesus over my mind and cast out every spirit*
> *of terror. Amen."*

5. Chucky – Spirit of Possessed Objects and Violence

Chucky represents the spirit of cursed or demon-possessed objects that open doors to violence and torment. This demon operates through fear, the manipulation of toys or items, and uncontrolled aggression—especially in children or vulnerable spaces.

> *"Lord, I break every curse attached to any object in my*
> *possession. I reject the spirit of violence and fear asso-*
> *ciated with cursed items. I command every unclean*
> *spirit tied to objects to leave now, in Jesus' name. I*
> *cleanse my home with the authority of Christ and*
> *declare it a place of peace and holiness. Amen."*

CHAPTER THIRTEEN
HAITIAN WITCHCRAFT

HAITIAN VODOU AND THE LOA

 Haitians traditionally practice Vodou (commonly spelled "Voodoo"), a religion that blends elements of African spirituality, Catholicism, and Indigenous Taíno beliefs. Central to Vodou is the veneration of spirits known as *Loa* (or *Lwa*).

Each Loa has distinct characteristics and is associated with specific aspects of life, nature, and human experiences.

For example:

- *Agwé:* The Loa of the sea, sailors, and fishermen; often honored by those seeking protection on the water.
- *Erzulie Freda:* The Loa associated with love, beauty, and prosperity.

- *Papa Legba:* A gatekeeper spirit who facilitates communication between humans and the spirit world.

Some well-known Loa include:

1. *Papa Legba:* The guardian of the crossroads and the spirit that facilitates communication between the living and the spirits.
2. *Erzulie Freda:* A spirit of love, beauty, and luxury, often associated with compassion and feminine energy. The goddess.
3. *Baron Samedi:* The spirit of the dead, who is often depicted in a top hat and glasses, representing the connection between life and death.
4. *Damballa:* A serpent spirit associated with creation, wisdom, and fertility, often depicted as a snake, unveiling the powers of African Deity.
5. *Ogun:* The spirit of iron, war, and labor, representing strength and resilience.

Vodou rituals often involve offerings, dances, and songs to honor the Loa and seek their guidance or blessings. It is a deeply spiritual practice that reflects the rich cultural heritage of Haiti and its people's connection to both the natural and supernatural worlds.

It's important to approach topics like Papa Legba and other spiritual entities with cultural sensitivity and respect, as they are integral to the spiritual and religious practices of many people. Haitian Vodou and African diaspora religions are not inherently malevolent or harmful; they are complex belief systems that reflect the history, resilience, and spirituality of their practitioners. Misrepresenting or demonizing these traditions can perpetuate harmful stereotypes.

If you are engaging in prayer or spiritual practices from a different belief system, it is essential to focus on your personal faith and intentions without disrespecting or vilifying other spiritual traditions. Below is a respectful and faith-based prayer for spiritual protection that does not directly target or demonize specific entities or spirits:

WARFARE PRAYER FOR SPIRITUAL PROTECTION

Heavenly Father,

I come before You in the name of Jesus Christ, my Lord and Savior. I thank You for Your love, grace, and mercy that sustain me every day. I seek Your protection and guidance as I navigate the spiritual challenges of this world.

Lord, I ask You to guard my heart, mind, and spirit against any influence that is not from You. Fill me with Your Holy Spirit, and let Your truth and light guide my path. I declare that no weapon formed against me shall prosper, and I stand firm in the victory won by Jesus Christ on the cross

Father, I ask for Your wisdom and discernment to recognize what is of You and what is not. Strengthen my faith and help me to remain steadfast in Your Word. I renounce any fear, confusion, or doubt, and I place my trust fully in Your power and promises.

Lord, I pray for peace and understanding between people of different beliefs and cultures. Help me to approach others with love and respect, just as You have commanded us to love one another.

Thank You for Your constant presence in my life and for

the assurance that You are greater than any challenge or obstacle I may face. I rest in Your protection and trust in Your unfailing love.

In Jesus' name, I pray.
Amen.

This prayer focuses on seeking protection and strength in your faith while fostering respect for others' beliefs. If you have specific concerns or questions about spiritual practices, consider consulting a trusted spiritual advisor or leader within your faith tradition for guidance.

WARFARE PRAYER AGAINST PAPA LEGBA SPIRITS

Heavenly Father,

I come before You in the name of Jesus Christ, seeking Your protection and guidance. I declare that You are the ultimate authority over all realms. I ask that You dispatch Your warring angels to guard me and my loved ones from any influence of spirits that seek to lead us astray.

I take authority over the spirit of Papa Legba and any spirits that dwell at the crossroads, believing that they serve as barriers to my communication and connection with You, Lord. I bind every unclean spirit that seeks to communicate false messages and lead souls into darkness.

In the name of Jesus, I cancel all assignments against me initiated by these entities. I render them powerless

*and void. Let the consuming fire of God surround me,
destroying every dark place and dispelling every false
spirit that seeks to come against me.*

*Father, I plead the blood of Jesus over my life and the lives
of my loved ones. I ask that You close all gateways and
entrances these spirits may attempt to use to infiltrate
our lives. Replace any fear with Your peace that
surpasses all understanding.*

*Guide me, Lord, to walk in Your path of righteousness. Let
my communication be solely directed by Your Holy
Spirit as I reject any influence from the realms of
darkness. I trust in Your protection and come boldly
before Your throne. I dwell in the secret place of the
Most High and abide under the shadow of the
Almighty, according to Psalm 91, declaring victory
over every attempt of the enemy.*

*Thank You, Lord, for hearing my prayer. I take hold of the
victory that is already mine through Christ Jesus.*

Amen.

ERZULIE FREDA

Erzulie Freda is a spirit of love, beauty, and luxury, often associated with compassion and feminine energy. Erzulie Freda is a prominent spirit in Haitian Vodou, often associated with love, beauty, and luxury. She represents compassion, romance, and is frequently called upon in matters of the heart. Erzulie Freda is also linked to wealth and prosperity, making her a figure for those seeking both emotional and financial fulfillment.

In Vodou practice, she is typically depicted as a beautiful woman who adores fine things, and she is known for her nurturing and protec-tive qualities. Devotees may invoke her for assistance in nurturing rela-tionships, enhancing beauty, and attracting love. Her followers often offer her gifts that reflect her love for luxury, such as perfumes, jewelry, and flowers.

Additionally, Erzulie Freda is sometimes viewed as a mother figure, embodying tenderness and care. She is seen as a guiding force in the lives of those who seek her assistance, offering support and blessings in their personal and emotional journeys.

WAREFARE PRAYERS AGAINST ERZULIE FREDA

I proclaim that "Christ redeemed us from the curse of the law by becoming a curse for us, for it is written: 'Cursed is everyone who is hung on a tree'" (Galatians 3:13).

In the name of the Lord Jesus Christ, I now bring the full-ness of His cross, death, blood, and sacrifice; His resurrection, life, and empty tomb; His authority, rule, and dominion. I bring judgment from the Lord Jesus Christ against every foul power, witchcraft, black art, and curse. I bring Jesus Christ, cursed for me, against all curses that have been raised against me—written, spoken, unspoken, or transferred to me.

[If you know what the exact curses are, it helps to name

them. For example, "all curses of death" or "all curses on my marriage or my health," etc.]

I bring the blood sacrifice of Jesus Christ, the Son of God, His blood shed upon the cross, against all blood sacrifices and rituals and their every claim against me.

I bring Jesus Christ, the Son of God, sacrificed for me, against all ritual sacrifices and their every claim against me.

I bring the dedication of Jesus Christ for me in death upon the cross against all ritual dedications.

In the name and by the blood of Jesus Christ, I break the power and hold of every curse that has come to me through ritual or ritual sacrifice.

In the name and by the blood of Jesus Christ, I break the power and hold of every curse that has come to me through transfer by another human being.

In the name and by the blood of Jesus Christ, I break the power and hold of every curse that has come to me through words spoken.

In the name and by the blood of Jesus Christ, I break the power and hold of every curse that has come to me through occult practices.

In the name of Jesus Christ, I declare every legal hold and every legal ground of the enemy broken, disarmed, and destroyed. Satan has no hold over me now through curses or occult practices, through sacrifices or any ritual of any kind. Through the blood of Jesus Christ, I am free. Thank You, Jesus, for setting me free. I order these curses and claims utterly disarmed and dismantled now, through the power of the blood of Jesus Christ and in His name.

In the name of Jesus Christ, I command all demonic spirits that have gained access to me through curses and rituals to be cut off and banished from me and my household, in the mighty name of the Lord Jesus Christ.

Jesus, I ask You to send Your angels now to completely disarm all curses and black arts from me; disarm their every device and render them destroyed. I ask Your angels to remove all foul spirits involved in these curses and black arts and bind them to Your feet for judgment.

I now claim every spiritual blessing that my Heavenly Father has given to me in Christ Jesus (Ephesians 1:3). I claim those blessings right here in the very place of all cursing, by the authority and power of the Lord Jesus Christ and in His name. Jesus, may these things be fully accomplished now through Your mighty name. I give You thanks and honor and praise.

All of this I pray by the authority and in the mighty name of the Lord Jesus Christ of Nazareth, who came in the flesh. Amen.

BARON SAMEDI

Baron Samedi is the spirit of the dead, often depicted wearing a top hat and glasses, symbolizing the connection between life and death. He is the leader of the Gede Loa group, the spirits of the dead in Vodou tradition. Bawon Samdi serves as the guardian of the barrier between the living and the dead, ensuring that the souls of the deceased pass safely into the afterlife.

He is often depicted as a tall, dark figure dressed in a top hat, black tuxedo, and sunglasses, with a skull for a face. Known for his mischievous and playful nature, Bawon Samdi should not be underestimated, as he holds the ultimate power over life and death.

Bawon Samdi is frequently invoked in rituals to communicate with the deceased. He is also believed to have the ability to heal the sick and protect against evil spirits.

The Gede Loa group includes other powerful spirits, such as Baron Lacroix, Baron Kriminel, Gede Nibo, Papa Gede, and Gede Mazaka, each with their own unique personalities and powers. Together, they form a vital part of Vodou's spiritual framework, bridging the realms of the living and the dead.

WARFARE PRAYER FOR BARON SAMEDI

Heavenly Father,

I come before You in humble prayer, seeking Your divine intervention against the powers of darkness. I recog-

nize that You are a God of light and truth, and that no weapon formed against me shall prosper.

In the name of Jesus, I bind the spirits of Bawon Samdi and Gede, and any plans they may have to harm or lead astray. I plead the Blood of Jesus over myself and my loved ones, proclaiming Your protection and deliverance.

Lord, I ask that You:

1. Disrupt their plans and render them powerless in my life.
2. Surround me with Your angels to guard and protect me from any malevolent forces.
3. Fill my heart with Your peace, and guide me in righteousness, away from any temptation or evil.

I declare victory in Your name, believing that You are greater than any power in this world. I claim the promise of Psalm 91:11, that You will command Your angels concerning me to guard me in all my ways.

Thank You, Lord, for Your everlasting protection and love.

In Jesus' name, I pray,
Amen.

DAMBALLA WÈDO AND AYIDA WÈDO

Damballa is a serpent spirit associated with creation, wisdom, and fertility, often depicted as a snake. Damballa Wèdo and Ayida Wèdo are the ultimate divine power couple in Vodou. They symbolize the

perfect balance and harmony of all creation, representing both masculine and feminine energies. Together, they are often depicted as two intertwined snakes, illustrating the union of their spirits.

Damballa is regarded as the original force of creation, believed to embody the inner voice of God. He is the source of all wisdom and knowledge and is associated with the serpent of the earth and the horizon.

Ayida Wèdo, on the other hand, is the rainbow, the serpent of the sky. She brings rain to nourish the earth and restores its beauty. Together, Damballa and Ayida represent the source of life and wisdom, embodying the interconnectedness of earth and sky, creation and renewal.

Their symbol, the intertwined snakes, is a powerful representation of their unity and is often seen on Vodou drums, furniture, and the *poto mitan* (the central pole of a peristyle, a sacred space used in Vodou rituals).

In many spiritual practices, including those involving the spirits Damballa Wèdo and Ayida Wèdo, it is important to approach prayer and intention with respect and an understanding of the traditions involved. In the context of Biblical prayer, you might consider focusing on themes of protection, deliverance, and healing.

On the following page, is a prayer you can adapt.

WARFARE PRAYER AGAINST DAMBALLA & AYIDA WÈDO

Heavenly Father,

I come before You in the name of Jesus, seeking Your divine protection and guidance. I ask for Your light to shine upon me and drive away any darkness that seeks to harm me.

Lord, I entrust my spirit to You. I pray that You break any chains of influence that Damballa Wèdo and Ayida Wèdo may have in my life. Surround me with Your angels and fill me with Your Holy Spirit.

In Your mighty name, I declare that any spirits contrary to Your will are bound and cast out from my life. I claim the victory You promised, for You are my refuge and fortress, my God in whom I trust.

Thank You, Lord, for Your protection and love. I trust in Your power to deliver me and fill me with peace.

Amen.

It is essential to approach spiritual matters with caution and ensure that your beliefs and practices align with your faith. If you are experiencing spiritual distress, consider seeking guidance from a trusted spiritual leader or counselor.

OGOU

Ogou, the mighty warrior Loa, embodies the spirit of strength, courage, and resilience. Much like the Roman war gods Mars and Jupiter, he commands both respect and fear from his followers. As a protector and guardian of his people, Ogou is associated with fire, the sword, and war.

He is a fierce and formidable deity with multiple manifestations, including Ogou Feray, Ogou Batala, and Ogou Badagri. Each form of Ogou has unique characteristics and attributes, yet all share a deep connection to war, the sword, and the forge. Known for his powerful energy and stern discipline, Ogou inspires those who seek to overcome their fears and transform into stronger, more resilient versions of themselves.

Ogou is said to embody the warrior spirit of the old *Oyo Empire* in West Africa. His *Vèvè* (sacred symbol) is associated with the emperors and kings who succeeded Abiodun, the legendary king of the Oyo people. Ogou's presence represents the enduring power of leadership, strength, and the indomitable will to fight for justice and progress.

WARFARE PRAYER AGAINST THE SPIRIT OF OGOU

Heavenly Father,

In the name of Jesus Christ, I come before you today to declare war against the spirit of Ogou, any influence it may have in my life, and any power it seeks to exert over me.

I stand firm in your authority and command this spirit to leave me completely, to be bound and cast out by the power of your Holy Spirit.

I break any curses, spells, or attachments related to Ogou that may be working against me, and I declare your protection over my life, mind, and spirit.

I choose to be filled with your light and strength, and I resist any attempts of darkness to infiltrate my life.

In Jesus' name,
Amen.

CHAPTER FOURTEEN

SPANISH WITCHCRAFT

Spanish witchcraft encompasses a wide range of traditions and practices, often influenced by local cultures, history, and beliefs. Below are five aspects:

1. *Brujería*: This term generally refers to witchcraft in Spanish-speaking cultures. It can include practices aimed at healing, protection, love, and even curses. Brujería often draws from indigenous, African, and European traditions.

2. *Curanderismo*: A traditional healing practice, curanderismo blends herbal medicine, spiritual guidance, and rituals. Curanderos (healers) often incorporate elements of Catholicism along with indigenous beliefs.

3. *Santería*: Although originating from Afro-Cuban traditions, Santería has influenced and interacted with various forms of witchcraft in Spain and Latin America. It combines African traditions with Catholicism and involves the worship of Orishas (deities) through rituals and offerings.

4. Folklore Magic: Each region in Spain (like Galicia, Andalusia, and Catalonia) has its own folk traditions, superstitions, and practices related to magic and witchcraft. These may involve charms, talismans, or rituals to ward off evil or attract good luck.

5. Modern Witchcraft: In contemporary Spain, Wicca and other neopagan movements have gained popularity, blending traditional beliefs with modern practices.

These practices can vary widely depending on the region, community, and individual beliefs.

BRUJERÍA

Brujería is term that broadly refers to witchcraft in Spanish-speaking cultures. Brujería encompasses a wide range of spiritual practices and rituals, often aimed at healing, protection, love, and, at times, curses. Rooted in the rich cultural tapestry of Latin America and the Caribbean, it draws influence from Indigenous, African, and European traditions, reflecting centuries of cultural blending and spiritual adaptation.

Practitioners of brujería, often called *brujos* (male practitioners) or *brujas* (female practitioners), may use herbs, candles, prayers, and sacred objects in their rituals. These practices can vary widely depending on the region and the specific traditions followed. Brujería is not inherently good or evil—it is a spiritual practice that can be used for various intentions, depending on the practitioner's goals.

Brujería often exists alongside other spiritual systems, such as

Santería, Curanderismo, and Catholicism, creating a unique blend of beliefs and practices. For many, it serves as a way to connect with their ancestors, seek guidance from spirits, and address the challenges of daily life through spiritual means.

WARFARE PRAYER AGAINST BRUJERÍA

In the name of Jesus Christ, I rebuke and break any curses, hexes, spells, demonic activity, or any other evil that has been sent against me.

Heavenly Father, I ask Your angels to remove all foul spirits involved in these curses and acts of darkness, and to bind them at Your feet for judgment.

I plead the shed blood of Jesus Christ, the Son of the Living God, over myself, my family, and all that I have lifted to You, Lord, as a shield of protection.

Thank You, Lord, for Your power, Your mercy, and Your everlasting love. I trust in Your authority and stand firm in Your victory. In Jesus' name, Amen.

CURANDERISMO

Curanderismo is a traditional healing practice that blends herbal medicine, spiritual guidance, and ritualistic practices. Curanderismo is a holistic approach to healing deeply rooted in the cultural traditions of Latin America. Practiced by *curanderos* (healers) or *curanderas* (female healers), it combines elements of indigenous beliefs, African influences, and Catholicism, creating a unique spiritual and medicinal system.

Curanderos often use natural remedies such as herbs, teas, and

oils to treat physical ailments, while also addressing emotional, mental, and spiritual imbalances through prayer, rituals, and energy work. Practices may include **limpias** (spiritual cleansings), **soul retrievals**, or the invocation of saints and spirits to intercede on behalf of the afflicted.

More than just a medical practice, curanderismo is a way of life for many, emphasizing the connection between body, mind, spirit, and community. It reflects a deep respect for nature, ancestral wisdom, and the divine, offering healing that transcends the physical and reaches into the spiritual realm.

WARFARE PRAYER AGAINST CURANDERISMO

> *Heavenly Father, I come before You with a heart full of faith, declaring Your Word as my weapon in this spiritual battle. As it is written in Psalm 7:15-16, I trust that every pit dug by the enemy will trap them instead. Let their mischief return upon their own heads.*

> *I declare, according to Psalm 35:8, that destruction will overtake those who seek my harm unexpectedly. Let the nets they have hidden ensnare them and lead them into their own downfall.*

> *In the spirit of Jeremiah 17:18, I ask that those who persecute me be confounded, while I remain steadfast. Let the day of evil fall upon them, and let their destruction be doubled.*

With the promise from Jeremiah 30:16-17, I proclaim that all who attempt to devour me will face their own demise. I stand firm in Your restoration of health and healing over my life.

Numbers 23:23 reminds me that no enchantment or divination can prosper against me, for I am covered by Your mighty hand. I declare that every adversary shall see what You have wrought in my life.

According to Psalm 18:44-45, I proclaim that as soon as they hear of me, they shall obey, and strangers shall submit themselves to me. Those who oppose me shall fade away in fear.

I embrace the power promised in Luke 10:19, standing confidently on Your Word, knowing that I tread over the enemy and his forces, unharmed.

As the axe is laid to the root in Matthew 3:10, I declare that every unfruitful tree in my life is cut down and cast into the fire.

With the assurance in Isaiah 41:10-12, I will not fear, for You are with me. All who oppose me shall be ashamed; those who strive against me will perish. I declare victory over every battle.

Isaiah 54:15,17 reassures me that those who gather against me shall fall for my sake, and no weapon formed against me shall prosper. I condemn every tongue raised against me, claiming my heritage as a servant of the Lord.

In accordance with Jeremiah 1:10,19, I take my stand over nations and kingdoms. The enemy may fight, but they will not prevail against me, for You are with me to deliver me.

In light of Obadiah 1:3-4, I know that the pride of those who oppose me will be their downfall, as You bring them low.

Isaiah 49:24-26 assures me that You will contend with those who contend with me and deliver my children. You will turn the tables on those who oppress, and all will know You as my Savior and Redeemer.

I claim Job 5:12, declaring that You will disappoint the devices of the crafty so they cannot succeed in the plans against me,

In Jesus Mighty Name,
Amen.

SANTERÍA

Santería is rooted in Afro-Cuban traditions. It is a syncretic spiritual practice that has significantly influenced and interacted with various forms of witchcraft and folk magic in Spain and Latin America.

FOLKLORE MAGIC

Each region in Spain, such as Galicia, Andalusia, and Catalonia, has its own unique folk traditions, superstitions, and magical practices.

These often involve charms, talismans, or rituals designed to ward off evil, attract good luck, or provide protection. Folklore magic is deeply rooted in local customs and reflects the cultural diversity of Spain, often blending ancient pagan traditions with Christian influences.

MODERN WITCHCRAFT

In contemporary Spain, Wicca and other neopagan movements have gained popularity, particularly among younger generations. These modern practices often blend traditional beliefs with New Age spirituality, incorporating elements like nature worship, moon phases, and ritual magic. This resurgence reflects a growing interest in reconnecting with ancestral traditions and exploring alternative spiritual paths.

These practices vary widely depending on the region, community, and individual beliefs, reflecting Spain's rich cultural and spiritual history.

CHAPTER FIFTEEN
AFRICAN WITCHCRAFT

African witchcraft encompasses a wide range of beliefs, practices, and traditions that vary significantly across different cultures and regions on the continent. These practices are often deeply rooted in the history and spirituality of various ethnic groups. Here are some common elements associated with witchcraft in Africa:

1. *Traditional Beliefs:* Many African communities hold belief systems that include ancestors, spirits, and the interconnectedness of all living things. Witchcraft is often viewed as a means of harnessing spiritual powers for various purposes.

2. *Healing and Medicine:* Traditional healers, often referred to as witch doctors or shamans, play a significant role in African societies. They may use herbal remedies, rituals, and divination to diagnose and treat illnesses, which can sometimes be mistakenly associated with witchcraft.

3. *Divination:* Various methods are used to communicate with

the spirit world or to seek guidance. This may include the use of objects, such as cowrie shells or bones, to predict the future or understand hidden truths.

4. *Community Practices:* Witchcraft can be both a communal and individual practice. It may involve rituals that seek the protection of the community or ceremonies designed to ward off malevolent forces.

5. *Magic:* Many African cultures incorporate the use of magic in their belief systems, including both beneficial (white magic) and harmful (black magic) practices.

6. *Rituals:* Ritual practices can include offerings, sacrifices, and ceremonies that aim to appease spirits, invoke protection, or seek justice.

7. *Social Control and Accusation:* In some societies, accusations of witchcraft can be used as a form of social control, allowing communities to deal with interpersonal conflicts or to explain misfortune.

It is essential to approach the topic of African witchcraft with respect and an understanding of the cultural contexts in which these beliefs and practices exist. They are deeply tied to identity, heritage, and the cohesion of communities, reflecting the rich spiritual diversity of the African continent.

WARFARE PRAYER AGAINST AFRICAN WITCHCRAFT

This prayer reflects a heartfelt appeal for spiritual protection and deliverance, rooted in Christian faith and scripture. It is a prayer of authority, renunciation, and intercession, calling upon God's power to nullify evil influences and protect oneself and others from harm.

Here's a breakdown of its key elements for deeper understanding:

1. Humility and Submission:
The prayer begins with a posture of humility, acknowledging God's authority and the believer's position in Christ. This aligns with the biblical principle of submitting to God before resisting the devil (James 4:7).

2. Renunciation of Evil:
The renouncement of curses, hexes, spells, and evil prayers reflects a rejection of any spiritual influence contrary to God's will. This act is rooted in the belief that Christ's sacrifice ("the blood of the Lamb") has the power to break all such bonds (Revelation 12:11).

3. Spiritual Warfare:
The prayer calls for the binding of demonic forces and the nullification of their assignments, reflecting the authority given to believers in Christ (Luke 10:19, Matthew 18:18).

4. The Law of the Thief:
This concept is drawn from Proverbs 6:31, where a thief must repay sevenfold. The prayer applies this principle spiritually, asking for any harm caused by curses or spells to return to the sender, not as vengeance but as a consequence of their actions, with the hope of leading them to repentance.

5. Intercession for the Opponent:
The prayer demonstrates compassion by asking God to reveal truth to those involved in occult practices, convicting them of sin (John 16:8) and leading them to salvation. This reflects Jesus' teaching to pray for one's enemies (Matthew 5:44).

6. Divine Protection:
By invoking God's heavenly warriors (angels), the prayer seeks protection for the individual, their family, and their surroundings. This aligns with biblical accounts of angelic intervention and protection (Psalm 91:11-12, Hebrews 1:14).

7. Faith in Christ's Victory:
The prayer concludes with a declaration of faith in Christ's victory over all evil (Colossians 2:15) and gratitude for this assurance. This reinforces the belief that the battle has already been won through Jesus' death and resurrection.

In Jesus Mighty Name,
Amen.

This prayer is a powerful expression of spiritual authority, faith, and reliance on God's protection. It also reflects a balance of standing firm against evil while interceding for the redemption of those who may be causing

CHAPTER SIXTEEN

MARINE SPIRITS

In various cultural beliefs and folklore, marine spirits are thought to be supernatural entities associated with water bodies, such as oceans, seas, and rivers. The effects of marine spirits on a person can vary widely depending on the specific cultural context. Here are some common themes:

1. *Spiritual Influence*: Some believe that marine spirits can influence a person's mental or emotional state. This could manifest as feelings of peace, calmness, or, conversely, restlessness and anxiety, depending on the spirit.

2. *Physical Health*: In some cultures, it's thought that marine spirits can affect a person's physical health, either by bringing good fortune and healing or by causing illness or misfortune.

3. *Behavioral Changes:* Individuals may experience changes in behavior, such as an affinity for water, an urge to engage in

aquatic activities, or sometimes, strange compulsions that may seem inexplicable.

4. Dreams and Visions: Encounters with marine spirits are sometimes said to occur in dreams or visions, leading to personal insights, warnings, or inspirations that influence one's life choices or perspectives.

5. Cultural Practices and Rituals: Many cultures have specific rituals, offerings, or practices intended to honor or appease marine spirits, aiming to gain their favor or protection.

6. Symbolism and Connection: For some, marine spirits symbolize a deep connection to nature, water, and the cycles of life, inspiring respect and reverence for aquatic environments.

It's important to note that perspectives on marine spirits are deeply rooted in folklore, spirituality, and personal beliefs, and experiences can vary widely among individuals and cultures. Here are a few examples of maritime spirits or entities thought to influence events at sea:

1. *Drowned Souls:* In some folklore, souls of those who have died at sea are believed to linger and may cause disturbances or accidents to warn others or seek revenge.

2. *Mami Wata:* In West African and Caribbean folklore, Mami Wata is a water spirit often associated with both benevolence and malevolence. Some stories suggest that she can bring both fortune and disaster, including maritime accidents.

3. *Mermaids:* Many cultures have tales of mermaids who lure sailors to their deaths. While they can represent beauty and

temptation, they are also seen as dangerous and potentially causing shipwrecks.

4. *Yara-Ma-Ya-Who*: A spirit from Brazilian folklore, this entity is associated with water and can manipulate the seas, sometimes leading to accidents or misfortunes.

5. *Krakens*: In Scandinavian folklore, the kraken is a legendary sea monster said to drag ships down to the depths, symbolizing the unpredictable and dangerous nature of the ocean.

These spirits and entities often serve as cultural explanations for the unpredictable and often dangerous nature of the sea and maritime travel. Always remember that beliefs about marine spirits can differ significantly from one culture to another.

WARFARE PRAYER AGAINST MARINE SPIRITS

Lord Jesus,

I come before You in the name of Jesus Christ, my Lord and Savior. I ask for Your divine protection and guidance. As I stand firm against the forces of darkness that rise like the great sea monster, I declare Your Word over my life and the lives of those I love.

In Revelation 13, we read of threats that seem insurmountable, but I am reminded that You are greater than any beast or spirit. I pray that You would send

Archangel Michael and Archangel Gabriel to guard me and keep me safe from all forms of evil, including the Kraken spirits that seek to drown my spirit in despair, fear, and chaos.

I renounce any influence these spirits may have over me or my household. I declare that their power is broken by the Blood of Jesus, and I command them to flee in His mighty name. I ask for Your knowledge, wisdom, and strength to navigate the waters of life, free from the grip of these dark forces.

Lord, fill me with Your Holy Spirit, illuminating my path and equipping me to stand strong. May Your truth anchor me, and may I always turn to You in times of trouble.

Thank You for Your love, protection, and the victory we have in Christ.

In Jesus' name,
Amen.

CHAPTER SEVENTEEN
SHAPESHIFTER SPIRITS

A shapeshifter is a figure or character in mythology, folklore, and fantasy literature that has the ability to change their physical form or appearance. Shapeshifters can take on the guise of animals, other people, or even inanimate objects. They are often depicted in various cultures as beings with magical or supernatural powers, and they can serve diverse roles ranging from tricksters to guardians.

In popular culture and fiction, shapeshifters may appear in movies, books, and television series, often exploring themes of identity, transformation, and the nature of reality. Some well-known examples include werewolves, witches, and characters in stories like "The Metamorphosis" by Franz Kafka or the X-Men series with characters like Mystique.

Yes, a shapeshifter can harm

someone in various ways, depending on the context of the story or mythology in which they exist. Here are a few common scenarios:

1. Deception and Manipulation:
Shapeshifters often use their ability to take on different forms to deceive others. By disguising themselves as someone trustworthy, they can manipulate their victims into making harmful decisions or betraying their allies.

2. Physical Attacks:
In many myths and stories, shapeshifters can transform into powerful or dangerous creatures, such as wolves, bears, or mythological beasts. In these forms, they may physically harm or even kill others.

3. Psychological Harm:
The ability to change appearance can create confusion, paranoia, or fear in others. For example, a shapeshifter might impersonate a loved one, causing emotional distress or mistrust within a group.

4. Curses or Magical Influence:
In some folklore, shapeshifters are associated with curses or dark magic. They may use their powers to place curses on others, bring misfortune, or influence events in harmful ways.

5. Stealing Identity or Resources:
By taking on the form of another person, a shapeshifter could steal their identity, possessions, or social status, leaving the victim powerless or ostracized.

6. Spreading Chaos:
As tricksters, some shapeshifters thrive on creating disor-

der. By switching forms and sowing lies or confusion, they can disrupt communities, relationships, or even entire kingdoms.

7. Predatory Behavior:

In certain tales, shapeshifters are predators who use their transformations to lure victims. For instance, some shapeshifters in folklore, like the selkie or kitsune, seduce or charm humans, only to harm them later.

8. Unintended Harm:

Not all harm caused by shapeshifters is malicious. In some stories, shapeshifters struggle to control their powers, inadvertently causing harm to those around them, such as transforming in a moment of rage or fear.

Shapeshifters are complex figures in mythology and fiction, often embodying themes of duality, deception, and transformation. Whether they are portrayed as villains, heroes, or morally ambiguous characters, their ability to change form makes them fascinating and unpredictable forces in storytelling.

WARFARE PRAYER AGAINST SHAPESHIFTERS

Here are some prayers you can use against shapeshifters, drawing on the biblical verses you've provided:

Prayer for Protection:

> *Lord, I come before You seeking Your protection against any evil forces that may try to deceive or harm me.*
>
> *According to Ephesians 6:11-13, I put on the full armor of*

*God, equipping myself with the belt of truth, the
breastplate of righteousness, and the shield of faith.*

*Help me to stand firm against the devil's schemes,
knowing that I am protected by Your power.*

Prayer of Submission and Resistance:

*Father, I submit my life to You, as James 4:7 encourages. I
resist any temptations or deceptions from the devil. I
stand firm in my faith and cling to Your promises,
knowing that You are with me.*

Prayer for Overcoming Evil:

*God of peace, I ask You to crush Satan under my feet, as
promised in Romans 16:20. Wherever the enemy seeks
to attack, I claim victory in Your name. I trust in Your
ability to provide me with the strength needed to overcome any dark forces.*

Prayer for Spiritual Warfare:

*Lord, according to 2 Corinthians 10:4-5, I wield the divine
weapons You provide, demolishing any strongholds of
the enemy. I pull down every argument and pretension that sets itself against Your knowledge. Fill me
with Your wisdom and discernment to recognize the
truth.*

Prayer for Vigilance:

*Help me to be sober-minded and watchful, as instructed in
1 Peter 5:8. I pray for alertness to spiritual dangers*

*and the courage to stand firm in my faith. Allow me to
see beyond appearances, focusing on Your truth.*

Prayer for Authority:

*Thank You, Jesus, for granting me authority, as stated in
Luke 10:19. I tread upon any serpents and scorpions
that come my way, knowing that I have power over all
the enemy's schemes. May Your light shine through
me, dispelling any darkness that seeks to infiltrate my
life.*

In Jesus' name, I pray. Amen.

CHAPTER EIGHTEEN
SEXUAL SPIRITS

A demon that flies through the air is often referred to as a "winged demon" or, in some contexts, a "flying demon." In various mythologies and folklore, such beings might also be associated with terms like "succubi," "incubi," or "fallen angels," depending on their traits and the specific cultural or religious context. In literature and popular culture, they may be given alternative names, such as "sky demon," or be identified by the names of specific demons from different mythologies.

INCUBUS

In folklore and mythology, an incubus is typically depicted as a male demon or spirit believed to engage in sexual activity with sleeping women. Their purpose is often described as seducing individuals, particularly at night, to satisfy their own desires. Incubi are frequently associated with themes of lust, desire, and, in some accounts, the draining of life force or energy from their victims.

In various cultural interpretations, incubi are also linked to nightmares and are sometimes used to explain phenomena such as sleep paralysis or other sleep disturbances. It is important to note that the concept of incubi is rooted in myth and superstition rather than empirical evidence or scientific reality.

Dealing with this spirit, I remembered that on January 8, 2025, I received a phone call from a dear friend who was struggling with demonic spirits. As I began to read Bible scriptures to ease her mind, the spirits started to manifest through loud burping sounds and gagging noises.

Now, remember, when you are about to approach these spirits, picture yourself in a field full of grass. You are wearing gloves to pull up unwanted weeds or trees that could choke your beautiful flowers, roses, or fruits. When you pull up those unwanted trees, you want to grab hold of the root to ensure they never grow back and choke your flowers again. Similarly, in the realm of the spirit, it is essential to get to the root of the issue—the source of what is holding that "tree" so firmly in the ground—and pull it up completely.

In the spiritual realm, demons often have strongholds over a person, keeping them in bondage. To free someone, you must go directly to the root of the problem to "uproot the tree." With this spirit, you would first want to discern, through the guidance of the Holy Spirit, how the demon gained access. Was it through a dream, generational lineage, or lust?

If the access is generational, you would need to break the curse from the 10th generation down. In other words, start by identifying and calling out the spirits tied to each generation as you count down from the 10th generation. Finally, seal every portal under the Blood of Jesus. Amen.

WARFARE PRAYER AGAINST INCUBUS

Heavenly Father,

I come before You today, seeking Your divine protection and strength. Your Word reminds me in Psalm 91:1-2 that "he who dwells in the secret place of the Most High shall abide under the shadow of the Almighty." Lord, I choose to dwell in Your presence, and I trust in You as my refuge and fortress.

I claim the promise of Ephesians 6:10-11, which calls us to "be strong in the Lord and in the power of His might." I put on the whole armor of God, that I may stand against the schemes of the enemy. Father, I ask for Your strength to help me resist and reject any dark spirits that come against me.

Your Word in 1 John 4:4 reassures me that "He who is in me is greater than he who is in the world." I declare that the power of Christ within me is greater than any evil force, and I assert that no evil spirit shall have authority over my life.

In the name of Jesus Christ, I command any incubus spirit or unclean spirit that seeks to harm me or bring unrest to flee. I ask for Your Holy Spirit and fire to fill my life, casting out all darkness and bringing peace to my mind, body, and spirit.

I take full authority, power, and dominion over every incubus spirit that has located me in my dreams or through generational lineage. In the mighty name of Jesus, I call you out NOW. Come out of my body NOW in the name of Jesus! Loose my mind, loose my understanding, loose my body, and loose me NOW in Jesus' name!

I command you to go back to the pit of hell from where you came and never return, in the name of Jesus Christ. Go back wherever Jesus sends you and never return to my life, my family's life, or my children's lives, in Jesus' name.

Lord, I thank You for Your unwavering love, protection, and deliverance. I trust in Your mighty power to deliver me from all harm and to keep me safe in Your embrace.

In Jesus' name, I pray.
Amen.

SUCCUBUS SPIRIT

A succubus spirit is a mythological or supernatural entity often described as a female demon or spirit believed to seduce men, typically while they sleep, through sexual activity or temptation.

The concept of the succubus has its origins in ancient folklore, mythology, and religious traditions and has been discussed in various cultures throughout history. Some characteristics of a Succubus Spirit are:

- *Sexual Seduction*: Succubi are often portrayed as highly seductive beings that attempt to engage in sexual acts with men, particularly during their sleep or in dreams.

- *Energy Draining:* Many traditions describe succubi as entities that drain the life force, energy, or vitality of their victims, leaving them feeling fatigued, weak, or spiritually compromised.

- *Symbol of Temptation*: Succubi are often symbolic representations of human struggles with lust, temptation, and sexual sin.

- *Appearance*: In mythology and folklore, succubi are often depicted as beautiful, alluring women, but some accounts describe them as having a demonic or monstrous form beneath their attractive exterior.

- *Connection to Sleep Paralysis*: Some interpretations link succubi to sleep paralysis, a condition where individuals feel paralyzed and may experience hallucinations of an oppressive or malevolent presence.

The term "succubus" comes from the Latin word succubare, meaning "to lie beneath," reflecting the idea of a spirit lying with or beneath a man during sleep. Succubi appear in various cultural traditions:

- In Jewish folklore, Lilith, Adam's first wife in some interpretations of the Genesis story, is sometimes associated with succubi.

- In medieval Christian demonology, succubi were

considered demons that tempted men into sin, particularly sexual immorality.

- In Islamic folklore, similar entities known as "qarin" or "jinn" are believed to tempt or harm humans.

* * *

The male counterpart to the succubus is the incubus, a male demon or spirit that seduces women, often in their sleep, and is also believed to drain their energy or harm them spiritually. Together, succubi and incubi are often associated with nocturnal spiritual attacks or demonic oppression.

In modern times, the succubus spirit is often viewed as a metaphor for struggles with sexual temptation, guilt, or spiritual warfare. In psychological terms, experiences attributed to succubi (or incubi) are sometimes explained as sleep paralysis, vivid dreams, or subconscious fears related to intimacy or sexuality.

From a spiritual or religious perspective, succubi are often regarded as unclean spirits or demonic entities that seek to lead individuals into sin, particularly through lust and sexual immorality. Many people who believe in the existence of succubi turn to prayer, spiritual warfare, and scripture to combat such attacks.

WARFARE PRAYER AGAINST SUCCUBUS SPIRIT

Heavenly Father,

I come before You today, seeking Your divine protection and strength. Your Word reminds me in Psalm 91:1-2 that "he who dwells in the secret place of the Most High shall abide under the shadow of the Almighty."

Lord, I choose to dwell in Your presence, and I trust in You as my refuge and fortress.

I claim the promise of Ephesians 6:10-11, which calls us to "be strong in the Lord and in the power of His might." I put on the whole armor of God, that I may stand against the schemes of the enemy. Father, I ask for Your strength to help me resist and reject any dark spirits that come against me.

Your Word in 1 John 4:4 reassures me that "He who is in me is greater than he who is in the world." I declare that the power of Christ within me is greater than any evil force, and I assert that no evil spirit shall have authority over my life.

In the name of Jesus Christ, I command any succubus spirit or unclean spirit that seeks to harm me or bring unrest to flee. I ask for Your Holy Spirit and fire to fill my life, casting out all darkness and bringing peace to my mind, body, and spirit.

I take full authority, power, and dominion over every succubus spirit that has located me in my dreams or through generational lineage. In the mighty name of Jesus, I call you out NOW. Come out of my body NOW in the name of Jesus! Loose my mind, loose my understanding, loose my body, and loose me NOW in Jesus' name!

I command you to go back to the pit of hell from where you came and never return, in the name of Jesus Christ. Go back wherever Jesus sends you and never return to my life, my family's life, or my children's lives, in Jesus' name.

Lord, I thank You for Your unwavering love, protection, and deliverance. I trust in Your mighty power to deliver me from all harm and to keep me safe in Your embrace.

In Jesus' name,
Amen.

CHAPTER NINETEEN
ALAMY SPIRITS

An Alamy spirit, also known as an "alam," is a term from various spiritual beliefs, particularly in some West African traditions. Typically, an Alamy spirit is considered a guiding or protective force related to an individual's spirituality or ancestry.

The specific roles and responsibilities of an Alamy spirit can vary based on cultural context, but generally, they are believed to:

- *Guide Individuals*: Alamy spirits can provide guidance and wisdom to individuals, helping them navigate life's challenges and making decisions.

- *Protect*: These spirits may offer protection against negative influences or harm, both physical and spiritual.

- *Connect with Ancestors*: Alamy spirits are often seen as a link between the living and the ancestral realm, helping individuals maintain a connection to their heritage.

- *Influence Well-being*: They may be called upon for assistance in promoting health, prosperity, and overall well-being.

- *Facilitate Communication*: In some traditions, Alamy spirits may assist in communication during rituals or spiritual ceremonies.

WARFARE PRAYER AGAINST THE ALAMY SPIRIT

Heavenly Father,

I come before You in the mighty name of Jesus Christ, seeking Your divine protection and deliverance from any Alamy spirit or unclean force that may be working against me. Your Word declares in Psalm 91:1-2 that those who dwell in the secret place of the Most High will abide under the shadow of the Almighty. Lord, I take refuge in You and declare that You are my fortress and my deliverer.

In the name of Jesus Christ, I take authority over every Alamy spirit or any spirit that seeks to harm me or my family. I command you to loose your grip and flee from my life now! You have no power, no authority, and no place in my life. I break every chain, curse, or stronghold that you have tried to establish, and I cast you out in the name of Jesus!

Lord, Your Word in Ephesians 6:12 reminds us that we wrestle not against flesh and blood, but against principalities, powers, and spiritual forces of evil in the heavenly realms. I put on the full armor of God—the helmet of salvation, the breastplate of righteousness, the belt of truth, the shield of faith, the sword of the Spirit, and the shoes of peace. I stand firm in the power of Your might, knowing that You have already won the victory.

I plead the blood of Jesus over my mind, body, and spirit. I declare that no weapon formed against me shall prosper, and every tongue that rises against me in judgment, I condemn, in the name of Jesus Christ.

Father, I ask You to send Your Holy Spirit to fill every void in my heart and life. Surround me with Your angels and cover me with Your protection. I declare that I am free, delivered, and victorious through the power of Jesus Christ.

In Jesus' mighty name,
Amen.

CHAPTER TWENTY

MOUNTAIN SPIRITS

The worship of demons or spirits in mountainous regions can vary greatly depending on cultural and regional beliefs. In many traditions, mountains are considered sacred places that may harbor spirits or deities. Here are a few examples of entities that might be worshiped in mountain areas:

1. *Mountain Spirits*: In various indigenous cultures, mountains are believed to be home to spirits or deities that protect the land and its people. These spirits might receive offerings or rituals in gratitude for their protection.

2. *Himalayan Deities*: In Hinduism and Buddhism, certain mountains are sacred, and specific deities associated with them, such as Shiva in the Himalayas, are revered. People might engage in rituals to gain favor or blessings.

3. *Local Folklore Figures*: Some cultures have local legends about demons or supernatural beings that inhabit the moun-

tains. Worship or rituals might be performed to appease these figures to ensure safety during journeys or harvests.

4. *Shamanic Practices:* In some indigenous cultures, shamans might engage with mountain spirits through rituals or offerings, asking for guidance or healing.

5. *Pagan Practices*: Certain neo-pagan traditions may include mountain worship, where natural elements are revered and rituals honor earth spirits or nature deities.

CHANTING IN VALLEYS AND NATURAL SETTINGS

Chanting in valleys or other natural settings often relates to various cultural or spiritual practices. Different people and traditions may have unique beliefs about demons, spirits, or deities associated with natural landscapes.

CHAPTER TWENTY-ONE
TRICKSTER SPIRITS

Some entities are known for causing mischief or confusion. A trickster spirit is often a figure in mythology, folklore, and religion that embodies qualities of deceit, mischief, and playfulness. These spirits serve various functions across different cultures, but generally share some common characteristics and roles:

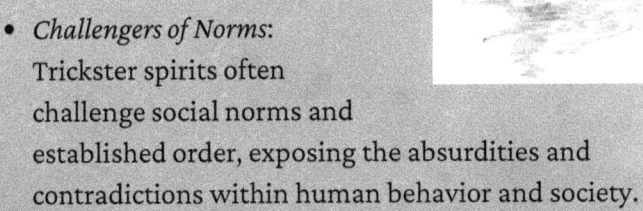

- *Challengers of Norms*:
  Trickster spirits often
  challenge social norms and
  established order, exposing the absurdities and contradictions within human behavior and society.

- *Bringers of Change*: They act as catalysts for transformation, using their cunning and wit to initiate change, which can be either positive or negative.

- *Humor and Playfulness:* Tricksters frequently use humor and playfulness to communicate their messages, teaching important lessons in a lighthearted or indirect manner.

- *Dual Nature*: Trickster spirits often possess a dual nature, combining both beneficial and harmful traits. While they can create chaos or confusion, they may also offer opportunities for growth, learning, or insight.

- *Symbols of Wisdom:* Despite their mischievous behavior, tricksters are sometimes seen as wise figures, using their cleverness and resourcefulness to navigate complex situations and teach valuable lessons.

Examples of trickster figures include Loki from Norse mythology, Anansi the Spider from African folklore, and Coyote from Native American traditions. Each of these figures reflects the characteristics described above in unique ways, often embodying the values and teachings of their respective cultures.

WARFARE PRAYER AGAINST A TRICKSTER SPIRIT

Heavenly Father,

I come before You today in the name of Jesus Christ, seeking Your protection and deliverance from any trickster spirit that seeks to cause confusion, mischief, or harm in my life. Lord, Your Word declares that You are not the author of confusion but of peace (1 Corinthians 14:33). I stand on this truth and ask You to remove any spirit of deceit, chaos, or distraction from my life.

In the mighty name of Jesus, I take authority over every trickster spirit operating against me. I bind and rebuke their influence, plans, and schemes. I declare that their attempts to sow confusion, division, or harm are nullified and rendered powerless.

Lord, Your Word in Isaiah 54:17 promises that no weapon formed against me shall prosper, and every tongue that rises against me in judgment will be condemned. I claim this promise over my life and rebuke any trickster spirit attempting to disrupt my peace, relationships, or purpose.

I ask You, Lord, to fill me with the Spirit of discernment so I may recognize and resist the deception of any trickster spirit. Surround me with Your divine protection, and let Your angels guard me in all my ways (Psalm 91:11).

Father, I also pray for wisdom and strength to navigate any challenges that may arise. Let Your Holy Spirit guide me in truth and clarity, so I may walk in alignment with Your will.

I plead the blood of Jesus over my mind, heart, and spirit, declaring that I am covered, protected, and victorious. Thank You, Lord, for Your faithfulness and for delivering me from all evil.

In Jesus' mighty name,
Amen.

CHAPTER TWENTY-TWO
PROTECTIVE SPIRITS

Protective spirits may be called upon for protection or to ward off negative energies. A protective spirit, often found in various spiritual and religious traditions, is believed to offer guidance, support, and protection from negative energies or influences. Below are some common functions attributed to protective spirits:

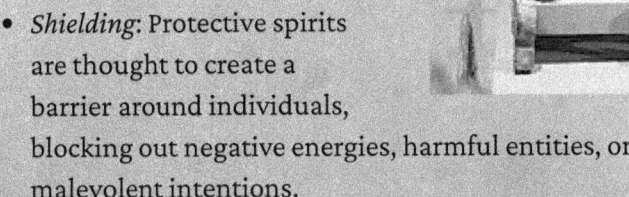

- *Shielding*: Protective spirits are thought to create a barrier around individuals, blocking out negative energies, harmful entities, or malevolent intentions.

- *Guidance*: They may provide wisdom and insight, helping individuals navigate difficult situations and make decisions aligned with their highest good.

- *Cleansing*: Some protective spirits are believed to assist in cleansing spaces or individuals of negative energies, fostering a more positive and harmonious environment.

- *Comfort*: These spirits often provide a sense of safety and reassurance, helping individuals feel supported and less isolated on their spiritual journey.

- *Intercession*: In certain beliefs, protective spirits may intercede on behalf of individuals, bringing blessings such as prosperity, health, and well-being by raising their vibrational frequency.

- *Awareness*: Protective spirits can heighten an individual's awareness of their surroundings, enabling them to recognize and avoid negative influences, harmful energies, or toxic relationships.

People may invoke the presence of protective spirits through prayer, rituals, meditation, or by calling upon specific symbols or names associated with these entities. Each tradition has its own unique practices for honoring and connecting with protective spirits.

WARFARE PRAYER AGAINST DEMONIC PROTECTIVE SPIRITS

Heavenly Father,

I come before You in the name of Jesus Christ, declaring Your authority and power over all principalities, powers, and spiritual forces of darkness. Your Word says in Ephesians 6:12 that we do not wrestle against flesh and blood but against spiritual forces of evil in the heavenly realms. Today, I stand firm in Your Word and take authority over every demonic spirit that masquerades as a protective force but seeks to deceive, harm, or lead me away from Your truth.

Lord, I rebuke and renounce every demonic spirit that has been invoked or allowed into my life, knowingly or unknowingly, under the guise of protection. I break every agreement, covenant, or connection with these spirits in the mighty name of Jesus Christ. I declare that You, Lord, are my one true protector, my shield, and my refuge, as written in Psalm 91:2: "I will say of the Lord, 'He is my refuge and my fortress, my God, in whom I trust.'"

In the name of Jesus, I bind and cast out every protective demonic spirit that seeks to guard or sustain strongholds of sin, fear, deception, or oppression in my life. I command them to leave me now and never return. I plead the blood of Jesus over my mind, body, and spirit, declaring that I am covered, cleansed, and made whole by His sacrifice.

Father, I ask that You fill every void left by these spirits with Your Holy Spirit. Surround me with Your heavenly angels, and let Your divine presence be my shield and fortress. I declare that no weapon formed against me shall prosper, and every tongue that rises against me in judgment shall be condemned (Isaiah 54:17).

Lord, I pray for discernment to recognize any counterfeit spirits that may try to deceive me. Let Your truth shine brightly in my life, exposing every lie and leading me into the fullness of Your light and love. I surrender

*myself completely to You, trusting in Your power to
protect and guide me.*

*Thank You, Lord, for the victory You have given me
through Jesus Christ. I stand firm in faith, knowing
that You are with me and that no force of darkness can
prevail against Your power.*

*In Jesus' mighty name,
Amen.*

CHAPTER TWENTY-THREE
ELEMENTAL SPIRITS

In some practices, practitioners may invoke spirits associated with the elements: earth, air, fire, and water.

Elemental spirits are often linked to the four classical elements: earth, air, fire, and water. In various spiritual, mythological, and metaphysical traditions, these spirits are believed to embody the qualities of their respective elements and perform specific functions or tasks. Below are some common roles attributed to elemental spirits:

- *Earth Spirits*: They are often associated with nature, growth, and stability. They are thought to promote fertility, healing, and grounding energies. Examples include gnomes and dryads.

- *Air Spirits*: They are connected to movement, intellect, and freedom. They are believed to inspire creativity, enhance communication, and encourage shifts in perspective. Sylphs are a common representation of air spirits.

- *Fire Spirits*: They typically embody passion, transformation, and energy. They represent willpower, motivation, and renewal, but they can also signify destruction. Salamanders are often regarded as spirits of fire.

- *Water Spirits*: They are linked to emotions, intuition, and purification. They are believed to influence feelings, aid in healing, and guide the flow of life. Examples of water spirits include undines and naiads.

In many traditions, elemental spirits are seen as guides or protectors, assisting humans in various ways. They may provide insights, enhance magical workings, or help harmonize with the natural world. Practitioners often invoke these spirits during rituals, meditation, or when seeking a deeper connection with nature.

PRAYER AGAINST ELEMENTAL SPIRITS

Heavenly Father,

I come before You in the name of Jesus. Thank You for the gift of salvation and the freedom I have in You. I recognize the struggles and influences of elemental spirits that may surround me. According to Your Word in Galatians 4:3 and 4:9, I do not want to be enslaved to anything that comes from this world.

Jesus, I ask for Your divine protection over my heart and

mind. Help me to discern the spirits at work around me, and grant me the strength to resist their influence. Fill me with Your Holy Spirit, and guide me toward the truth that sets me free.

In the name of Jesus, I bind any elemental spirits that seek to lead me away from Your love and truth. I declare that I am a child of God, redeemed and set free by Your grace. Thank You for Your faithfulness, and help me to walk in the freedom You have given me.

In Jesus' mighty name,
 Amen.

CHAPTER TWENTY-FOUR
DJINN SPIRIT

In various cultures and mythologies, particularly in Arabic and Islamic traditions, djinn (or genies) are supernatural beings created from smokeless fire. They are believed to possess free will, much like humans, and can be good, evil, or neutral. Below are some key points about djinn spirits and their roles:

- *Influence and Interaction:* Djinn are thought to interact with the human world in various ways. They can influence human thoughts and actions and may provide guidance or temptation.

- *Granting Wishes:* In popular culture, djinn are often depicted as wish-granters, similar to the fairy tale interpretation of the genie in a lamp. However, in traditional beliefs, the granting of wishes is far more complex and often comes with unforeseen consequences.

- *Shape-shifting:* Djinn are known for their ability to change shape, taking on various forms, including animals or even humans.

- *Habitat:* Djinn are believed to inhabit desolate places such as deserts, ruins, and caves. They can sometimes be summoned through specific rituals.

- *Spiritual Lessons:* In some beliefs, djinn serve as a test of human character or morality, teaching lessons about desires and their consequences.

- *Protection and Mischief:* Some djinn are considered guardians or protectors, while others may engage in mischievous or malevolent behavior, causing harm or chaos.

Overall, djinn are complex beings with a wide range of roles and attributes across various belief systems. Their portrayal varies significantly, from traditional folklore to modern fiction.

SCRIPTURES TO DEFEAT THE DJINN SPIRIT

- "Do not conform to the pattern of this world, but be transformed by the renewing of your mind. Then you will be able to test and approve what God's will is—his good, pleasing, and perfect will." — Romans 12:2 (NIV)

- "Do not be anxious about anything, but in every situation, by prayer and petition, with thanksgiving, present your requests to God. And the peace of God, which transcends all understanding, will guard your hearts and your minds in Christ Jesus." — Philippians 4:6-7 (NIV)

- "Set your minds on things above, not on earthly things. For you died, and your life is now hidden with Christ in God." — Colossians 3:2-3 (NIV)

- "But the Lord is faithful, and he will strengthen you and protect you from the evil one." — 2 Thessalonians 3:3 (NIV)

- "When I said, 'My foot is slipping,' your unfailing love, Lord, supported me. When anxiety was great within me, your consolation brought me joy." — Psalm 94:18-19 (NIV)

WARFARE PRAYER AGAINST DJINN SPIRITS

Heavenly Father,

I come before You and ask for Your divine protection. I stand firm in my faith, rejecting any influence or attack from djinn spirits or any negative forces. I claim the promise of Your peace, as stated in Philippians 4:6-7, knowing that You guard my heart and mind through Christ Jesus. I set my mind on things above, as instructed in Colossians 3:2, and I trust in Your faithfulness to strengthen and protect me from evil, as declared in 2 Thessalonians 3:3. Surround me with Your love and support, as stated in Psalms 94:18-19, comforting me in times of anxiety.

In the name of Jesus, I take authority over every shape-shifting spirit of djinn and command you to go back to the pits of hell from where you came. You are never to return to me, my family, or my friends, in Jesus' name. I cancel your assignments, plots, and schemes, and I call upon the Lord Jesus Christ to send you wherever He wills.

In Jesus' mighty name,
Amen.

CHAPTER TWENTY-FIVE
LILITH SPIRIT

The Lilith spirit is often associated with various interpretations across different cultures and belief systems.

In folklore and mythology, Lilith is frequently depicted as a figure of independence, femininity, and, at times, rebellion.

Below are some common themes related to the Lilith spirit:

- *Feminine Empowerment*: Lilith is often seen as a symbol of women's empowerment, representing autonomy and the rejection of traditional gender roles.

- *Transformation*: The Lilith spirit is sometimes associated with transformation and change, encouraging individuals to embrace their true selves and break free from societal constraints.

- *Shadow Work*: In psychological and spiritual contexts, the Lilith spirit can represent the darker aspects of the psyche, prompting personal introspection and the healing of deep-seated issues.

- *Sexuality and Desire*: Lilith is frequently connected with sexuality, desire, and sensuality, serving as a reminder of the importance of embracing and owning one's desires.

- *Rebellion*: In many stories, Lilith is portrayed as a rebellious figure who defies authority, inspiring independence and a willingness to challenge the status quo.

The interpretation of the Lilith spirit varies widely depending on the cultural, spiritual, or psychological lens through which she is viewed.

WARFARE PRAYER AGAINST THE SPIRIT OF LILITH

Heavenly Father,

I come before You, acknowledging Your sovereignty and power over all creation. Your Word says in Psalm 127:1, *"Unless the Lord builds the house, those who build it labor in vain."* I invite You into my life and my home to be the foundation and protector against any harmful spirits, including the spirit of Lilith.

Lord, I ask for Your divine protection over my family and loved ones. Shield us from any influences that seek to bring chaos, fear, or destruction. Fill our home with

Your peace and presence, and let Your light dispel all darkness.

I pray for wisdom and strength to discern any negative energies and to stand firm in Your truth. Grant us the courage to seek You in all matters and to trust in Your plan for our lives.

You are our refuge and fortress. I commit every aspect of my life into Your hands. May Your love and grace reign in my heart and in my home.

In Jesus' name,
Amen.

CHAPTER TWENTY-SIX

BAAL SPIRIT

The demon often associated with causing accidents, including car, boat, and plane accidents, is known as "Baal." In various mythologies and demonologies, Baal is sometimes depicted as a figure who influences chaos and misfortune. However, specific names and characteristics can vary depending on folklore or belief systems. If you're interested in a particular culture's interpretation, please let me know!

Baal is a powerful spirit in various occult traditions, often associated with the practice of demonology. The term "Baal" comes from ancient Near Eastern religions, where Baal was a deity associated with fertility, weather, rain, and agriculture.

In modern occult practices, particularly in systems like the Goetia (part of "The Lesser Key of Solomon"), Baal is considered a high-ranking demon or spirit.

Here are some aspects typically associated with Baal in these contexts:

- *Rank*: Baal is often described as a king among demons, commanding numerous legions of spirits.

- *Abilities*: In demonology, he is said to possess various abilities, including the power to grant knowledge, control over storms, and influence people's personalities or decisions.

- *Nature*: Baal is generally depicted as a spirit of chaos and destruction, but he can also bring about beneficial changes depending on the practitioner's intentions and the context of the ritual.

- *Invocation*: Ritual practitioners who seek to work with Baal often perform specific invocations to summon his presence and request assistance.

- *Symbolism*: In some interpretations, Baal symbolizes the chaotic forces of nature, as well as the potential for transformation and change within one's life.

As with any spirit or entity in occult practices, working with Baal requires caution, respect, and an understanding of the potential risks involved. Always approach such practices with care and thorough research.

In 1 Kings 18:25-29, the prophet Elijah confronts the prophets of Baal on Mount Carmel. The context of these verses involves a dramatic showdown where Elijah challenges the prophets of Baal to call upon their god to consume a sacrifice with fire. The passage illustrates the futility of worshiping Baal and the power of the true God.

Overview of 1 Kings 18:25-29:

- *Challenge*: Elijah tells the prophets of Baal to prepare a bull for sacrifice and call upon their god to send fire.
- *Desperation*: The prophets of Baal call out, dance, and cut themselves, trying to gain Baal's attention, but there is no response.
- *Mocking*: Elijah humorously mocks them by suggesting that maybe Baal is meditating, busy, or on a journey.

WARFARE PRAYER TO DESTROY THE BAAL SPIRIT

Heavenly Father,

We come before You today, acknowledging Your sovereignty and power. Just as Elijah called upon You on Mount Carmel, we ask for Your presence to be felt mightily among us. We renounce the spirit of Baal, which seeks to distract, deceive, and turn hearts away from You.

Lord Jesus, we pray that You would expose any idols in our lives and in our communities. Help us to recognize the false gods that seek our devotion—be it materialism, pride, or anything that stands in opposition to Your truth.

We ask for the fire of Your Holy Spirit to consume these

*idols and cleanse our hearts. Let Your truth reign
supreme in our lives, and may we worship You in
spirit and in truth.*

*As we turn our hearts back to You, we trust in Your power
to deliver us from all bondage, and we declare that
You alone are God. May Your glory be revealed, and
may every spirit of Baal be cast out.*

*In Jesus' mighty name,
Amen.*

CHAPTER TWENTY-SEVEN
JEZEBEL SPIRIT

 The term "Jezebel Spirit" is often used in Christian circles to describe a spirit or influence that embodies manipulation, seduction, and rebellion against God's authority. It is named after Queen Jezebel from the Bible, who is portrayed in the Old Testament (1 Kings 16-21) as a Phoenician princess who married King Ahab of Israel.

Jezebel is often associated with idolatry, immorality, and the persecution of God's prophets, particularly the prophet Elijah. In modern discussions, the "Jezebel Spirit" may be described as a force that seeks to control, undermine authority, and lead others away from God through deceitful tactics.

People who refer to a "Jezebel Spirit" may believe it represents characteristics such as:

1. *Manipulation*: Using charm or deceit to influence others for personal gain.

2. *Seduction*: Engaging in provocative behavior to draw people away from their commitments or beliefs.

3. *Rebellion*: Opposing authority, particularly in spiritual or church contexts.

4. *Division*: Causing strife and separation among people, often to weaken or disrupt communities or relationships.

It's important to note that interpretations of the "Jezebel Spirit" can vary widely among different religious groups, and the concept is sometimes used metaphorically in broader cultural contexts.

DECLARATIONS TO BREAK THE SPIRIT OF JEZEBEL

1. I loose the hounds of heaven against Jezebel (1 Kings 21:23).
2. I rebuke and bind the spirits of witchcraft, lust, seduction, intimidation, idolatry, and whoredom connected to Jezebel.
3. I release the spirit of Jehu against Jezebel and her cohorts (2 Kings 9:30–33).
4. I command Jezebel to be thrown down and eaten by the hounds of heaven.
5. I rebuke all spirits of false teaching, false prophecy, idolatry, and perversion connected with Jezebel (Rev. 2:20).
6. I loose tribulation against the kingdom of Jezebel (Rev. 2:22).
7. I cut off the assignment of Jezebel against the ministers of God (1 Kings 19:2).

WARFARE PRAYER AGAINST JEZEBEL

In the name of Jesus, I command every spirit of Jezebel operating around my ministry to scatter by the consuming fire of God. You spirit of Jezebel, hear the Word of the Lord: "No weapon formed against me shall prosper, and every tongue that rises against me in judgment is condemned" (Isaiah 54:17).

In Jesus' mighty name, I break your strongholds of witchcraft, lust, seduction, intimidation, idolatry, and whoredom. According to Ephesians 6:12—"For we wrestle not against flesh and blood, but against principalities, powers, rulers of the darkness of this world, and spiritual wickedness in high places"—I take authority over you now.

By the power of Jesus Christ, I weaken your forces and your influence over my ministry and every ministry connected to me. I release the spirit of Jehu against you in Jesus' name. I rebuke and uproot every demonic force sent against my ministry—false teachings, false prophecies, and perversion—connected to your works, Jezebel.

I dismantle every assignment you have planned against my ministry and the ministries I am connected to, in the mighty name of Jesus. I send confusion and shame into your camp, and let every plan meant for my harm fall back upon your own head sevenfold in Jesus' name.

I plead the blood of Jesus over myself, my family, and every person affected by the spirit of Jezebel. I decree and declare total victory in Jesus' mighty name.

In the mighty name of Jesus,
Amen.

CHAPTER TWENTY-EIGHT

MARA SPIRIT

The demon you might be referring to is often called a "nightmare" or "sleep paralysis demon." In folklore, some cultures specifically refer to a creature known as a "Mara," which is said to sit on your chest while you sleep, causing feelings of fear and suffocation. This phenomenon can be linked to sleep paralysis, where a person is temporarily unable to move or speak while falling asleep or waking up.

In various mythological and religious traditions, particularly within Buddhism, the Mara demon is often associated with temptation and distraction from spiritual practice. Mara personifies the obstacles and challenges that can hinder individuals on their path to enlightenment.

These include:

1. *Temptation*: Mara tries to seduce individuals with pleasures and worldly distractions to keep them from pursuing spiritual goals.

2. *Fear*: Mara represents doubts and fears that arise in one's mind, discouraging individuals from progressing in their spiritual journey.

3. *Distraction*: Mara embodies the distractions of everyday life that can divert focus from meditation and mindfulness.

WARFARE PRAYER AGAINST MARA SPIRITS

Heavenly Father,

I come before You today, acknowledging Your sovereignty over all creation, as declared in Genesis 1:1-31, where You spoke the world into existence and pronounced it good. I praise You for Your mighty power and authority.

Lord, just as You sent Ruth back to her people and provided for her in her time of need (Ruth 1:1-22), I ask that You lead me away from the bitterness and despair that Mara represents. Help me to remember that Your plan for my life is still "Yes" and "Amen," just as it was for Ruth, and that You can turn my mourning into joy.

In Malachi 3:1, You promise to send a messenger to purify and refine. Oh Lord Jesus, I ask for Your refining fire to cleanse me from any negative spirits, especially the Mara spirits that seek to steal my joy and hope. Protect my heart and mind from bitterness and despair, and fill me with Your love and peace.

Lord, I declare that I am a new creation in Christ, and I choose to walk in the victory that You have won for me. Help me to release any negative thoughts, frustrations, anger, or hurts, and to embrace Your healing and restoration.

Thank You, Father, for the hope I have in You. I trust that You are working all things together for my good. I claim victory over every Mara spirit in my life and declare that I am free to live in Your joy and abundance.

In Jesus' name,
Amen.

CHAPTER TWENTY-NINE
MIRROR SPIRIT

A mirror demon forms as a familiar spirit to make the person comfortable. It is often a character found in folklore, fantasy litera- ture, or horror stories, typically associated with themes of reflection, identity, and deception. While specific definitions can vary, here are some common traits and roles associated with mirror demons:

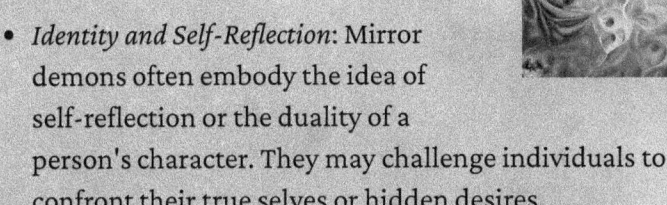

- *Identity and Self-Reflection*: Mirror demons often embody the idea of self-reflection or the duality of a person's character. They may challenge individuals to confront their true selves or hidden desires.

- *Illusions and Deception*: These beings are frequently depicted as tricksters that can manipulate reality, creating illusions or alternate versions of individuals.

They may confuse or mislead others by showing distorted reflections of themselves or others.

- *Guardians of Secrets*: In some stories, mirror demons serve as guardians of knowledge or secrets, only revealing truths to those who can solve riddles or prove their worthiness.

- *Curses and Transformations*: Encountering a mirror demon may lead to curses, such as being trapped in a mirror or undergoing a transformation, often teaching a lesson about vanity or self-acceptance.

- *Horror Elements*: In horror narratives, mirror demons can invoke fear by representing inner fears or unacknowledged aspects of one's personality, often manifesting as terrifying or grotesque versions of the characters.

Overall, mirror demons serve various symbolic purposes, often representing the complex relationship individuals have with their identities and the truths they might wish to avoid confronting.

MIRROR DEMONS AND DEMENTIA

Communicating with a person with dementia can be challenging due to the cognitive and memory impairments involved. If we consider a "mirror demon" as a fictional concept or character that serves as a symbol of their inner struggles, the interaction could focus on employing gentle, compassionate communication strategies. Here are some approaches to facilitate connection:

1. *Reflective Listening*: The mirror demon could mirror back what the person with dementia says, validating their feelings and experiences without correcting them. Simple responses that show understanding can be helpful.

2. *Nonverbal Communication*: Using gestures, facial expressions, and body language can be effective. The mirror demon could use calming actions to convey empathy and emotional understanding.

3. *Simple Language:* Communication should be clear and straightforward. The mirror demon might use short sentences and familiar words to make it easier for the person to understand, such as, "Come, let's go back to your house," or, "Why are these people here? Chase them out."

4. *Memory Cues:* The mirror demon could help trigger memories by gently bringing up familiar places, people, or experiences that may resonate with the individual, such as mentioning an old friend, deceased parents, or a family member who has passed away.

5. *Stay Patient and Calm:* A calm demeanor can help reduce anxiety. The mirror demon could embody a peaceful presence to help create a safe space for communication by saying things like, "You look pretty today."

6. *Engaging in Activities*: Instead of direct conversation, the mirror demon might engage the person in simple activities they enjoy, such as listening to music or looking through old

photographs, which can prompt memories and facilitate connection.

Overall, the focus should be on creating a sense of safety and acceptance, allowing the individual with dementia to express themselves in a way that is comfortable for them.

When seeking a prayer for healing, especially for conditions like dementia, it can be helpful to draw on scripture for inspiration and comfort. Here are a couple of scriptural prayers you can consider:

1. Prayer for Healing and Peace:

> *Lord, I come before You, asking for healing for [Name] who is suffering from dementia. Your Word tells us in Psalm 147:3, "He heals the brokenhearted and binds up their wounds." I pray that You will bind up their mind and restore their memory. Grant them peace that surpasses all understanding (Philippians 4:7) during this time.*

2. Prayer for Wisdom and Strength:

> *Heavenly Father, I ask for Your wisdom and strength for [Name] and their caregivers. In James 1:5, You tell us to ask for wisdom, and You will give it generously. Grant them understanding and comfort, and help them to feel Your love and presence daily. May your healing touch bring restoration and hope.*

3. Prayer for Remembering:

> *God, I pray for [Name] to remember the good things in their life as You remind us in Isaiah 46:4, "Even to your old age and gray hairs I am he, I am he who will*

sustain you." May they feel your presence and love, and allow Your spirit to bring clarity to their mind.

SCRIPTURAL PRAYER AGAINST ANXIETY

Heavenly Father,

I come before You in the name of Jesus, seeking Your divine protection and peace. I feel the weight of anxiety as I confront the fear of the mirror demon. Your Word reassures me that I am not alone.

"Cast all your anxiety on Him because He cares for you." (1 Peter 5:7)

Lord, I surrender my fears and anxieties to You. I ask for Your strength to overcome this darkness.

"For God has not given us a spirit of fear, but of power and of love and of a sound mind " (2 Timothy 1:7)

In Jesus' name, I declare that I have power over any spirit that seeks to instill fear. I stand firm in the truth of Your Word and claim the promise of Your protection.

"The Lord is my light and my salvation—whom shall I fear?" (Psalm 27:1)

I ask that You surround me with Your angels to guard me from any evil influences. Let Your light dispel any darkness around me and within me.

"You will keep in perfect peace those whose minds are steadfast because they trust in You." (Isaiah 26:3)

Help me to trust in Your goodness, Lord. I seek Your perfect peace to fill my heart and mind.

Thank You for Your love and protection. I rest in the assurance that I am safe in Your presence.

In Jesus' name,
Amen.

CHAPTER THIRTY
MET AGWE TAWOYO

Met Agwe is a powerful spirit of the oceans. He is the ruler and guardian of its bounties. He is often compared to the Greek god Poseidon and is beloved by fishermen and sailors for his generous spirit. His mythical residence, Nan Zile, is said to be hidden deep in the sea's depths.

During Vodou rituals, those possessed by Met Agwe often turn toward the sea, acknowledging his powerful presence. He is married to Mambo La Sirène, the Haitian mermaid, and together they rule over a large group of spirits in the Vodou pantheon.

WARFARE PRAYER AGAINST MET AGWE

*I call upon Jehovah El-Gibbor, my God of War, to come
and fight this battle for me in the name of Jesus.*

*Dear Lord, I seek Your divine protection as I face the
powers of darkness. I ask that You surround me with
Your heavenly armor and shield me from any harm or
negativity. As Psalm 91:1-2 states, "He who dwells in
the secret place of the Most High shall abide under the
shadow of the Almighty. I will say of the Lord, 'He is
my refuge and my fortress, my God, in whom I trust.'"*

*Almighty God, I call upon Your strength to overcome the
challenges posed by Met Agwe. I lean on the assurance
from Philippians 4:13, that "I can do all things
through Christ who strengthens me." Be my anchor in
the stormy seas of conflict.*

*So, in the name of Jesus, I ask for Your deliverance from
any ties or bondages that Met Agwe may have over
my life. According to Psalm 34:17, "The righteous cry
out, and the Lord hears them; He delivers them from
all their troubles." I claim this promise of freedom in
Your name.*

*God, grant me the wisdom to navigate the influences of
these spirits. As James 1:5 teaches us, 'If any of you
lacks wisdom, let him ask of God, who gives to all
liberally and without reproach, and it will be given to
him.' Fill me with discernment and clarity during this
spiritual battle.*

Lord, I yearn for Your peace within my heart as I confront the spirit of Met Agwe. Philippians 4:6-7 encourages me, "Do not be anxious about anything, but in every situation, by prayer and petition, with thanksgiving, present your requests to God. And the peace of God, which transcends all understanding, will guard your hearts and your minds in Christ Jesus." May Your peace envelop me.

Thank You, wonderful Father, for delivering me out of the hands of Met Agwe.

In Jesus' Mighty Name.
Amen.

CHAPTER THIRTY-ONE
MANBO LASIREN DYAMAN

Manbo Lasiren Dyaman is the wife of Met Agwe. In the world of Haitian Vodou, the mermaid goddess of the sea, Lasiren, reigns supreme. With her alluring half-woman, half-fish form, she embodies the wealth and abundance of the ocean and is revered as a powerful Loa who can grant prosperity and good fortune to her followers.

As the wife of Met Agwe, she rules over the vast kingdom of the oceans with him. According to Haitian culture, whoever finds her comb will become the master of immense wealth. But beware—Lasiren isn't just a benevolent spirit. When angered, she can be fickle and dangerous. In her alternate form of Labalenn, the whale, she can manifest as a powerful force of unconsciousness.

WARFARE PRAYER AGAINST LASIREN

Heavenly Father,

As I come before You today, I seek Your guidance and strength. Just as Revelation 17:1 speaks of the judgment upon those who lead others astray, I ask for Your wisdom to recognize and combat any negative forces in my life, including the influence of Lasiren.

Lord, according to Nahum 3:1-3, we know that violence, deceit, and destruction will not stand before Your justice. I pray for Your protection over myself and my loved ones from any harm that may come our way. Help me to stand firm in my faith, trusting in Your might to overcome the adversities we face.

I ask that You expose the works of darkness and render them powerless. May Your truth shine brightly, destroying all deception and revealing a path of light and righteousness. Equip me with spiritual armor to fend off any attack that attempts to disrupt my peace.

In the authority of Jesus' name, I declare victory over every oppressive influence. May justice roll like a river and righteousness like a never-failing stream. Let any evil monitoring mirror ever used against me under any water crash to irredeemable pieces, in the name of Jesus.

Every marine witchcraft that has introduced a spirit husband, wife, or child in my dreams, be roasted by fire, in the name of Jesus.

*Every agent of marine witchcraft physically attached to
my marriage to frustrate it, fall down and perish now,
in Jesus' name.*

*Every agent of marine witchcraft assigned to attack my
fiancé through dreams, fall down and perish, in the
name of Jesus.*

*I file a counter report in heaven against every water spirit,
in the name of Jesus.*

*I pull down every stronghold of bewitchment, enchant-
ment, jinx, or divination fashioned against me by
marine witches, in the name of Jesus.*

*Let the thunderbolts of God locate and destroy every
marine witchcraft coven where deliberations and
decisions have ever been fashioned against me, in the
name of Jesus.*

*Any water spirits from my village or place of my birth,
practicing witchcraft against me and my family, be
amputated by the word of God, in the name of Jesus.*

*Let every spiritual weapon of wickedness fashioned
against me under any river or sea be roasted by the
fire of God, in the name of Jesus.*

*Any power of marine witchcraft holding any of my bless-
ings in bondage, receive the fire of God and release
them, in Jesus' name.*

*I loose my mind and soul from the bondage of marine
witches, in the name of Jesus.*

*Any marine witchcraft chain binding my hands and feet
   from prospering, be broken and shattered to pieces, in
   the name of Jesus.*

*Every arrow shot into my life from under any water by
   witchcraft powers, come out of me and go back to your
   sender, in the name of Jesus.*

*Any evil material transferred into my body through
   contact with any marine witchcraft agent, be roasted
   by fire, in the name of Jesus.*

*Every sexual pollution of a marine spirit husband or wife
   in my body, be flushed out by the blood of Jesus
   right now.*

*Thank You, Lord, for Your unfailing love and protection. I
   trust that You are working all things for my good.*

*In the mighty name of Jesus,
Amen.*

CHAPTER THIRTY-TWO
KOUZEN ZAKA

Known as the quintessential farmer Loa, Kouzen Zaka is beloved by rural communities for his ability to ensure a bountiful harvest and prosperity in the fields. He is often depicted wearing a straw hat and carrying a machete and a djakout (woven grass bag). Celebrated every May 1st  during the Feast of Agriculture and Work, he is known to oppose laziness and idleness.

Kouzen Zaka is a friend to hardworking people, granting them success in their labors. He is often associated with Saint Isidore of Seville and loves all Haitians, living or dead. With a childlike version of himself called Ti-Zaka in some lineages, this lovable Loa is all about embracing the power of hard work.

WARFARE PRAYERS AGAINST KOUZEN ZAKA

Prayer based on Romans 6:11-14):

> *Dear Lord, I come before You, acknowledging my union with Christ in His death and resurrection. Help me to consider myself dead to sin and alive to You. I ask for strength to resist all forms of darkness, including the influence of Kouzen Zaka, which might lead me away from Your light. Let Your grace reign in my life, guiding my choices and actions. May I offer myself to You, not yielding to the demands of sin but living in Your righteousness. Amen.*

Prayer based on Galatians 2:20:

> *Heavenly Father, I thank You that I have been crucified with Christ, and it is no longer I who live, but Christ who lives in me. I pray that Your Spirit empowers me to live boldly and faithfully in the face of all adversities, including the challenges presented by Kouzen Zaka. Let my life reflect Your love and strength each day. As I walk in faith, may I always remember to lean on Your everlasting arms. Amen.*

Prayer based on Hebrews 3:15:

> *Gracious God, as it is said, 'Today, if you hear His voice, do not harden your hearts.' I open my heart to Your Word and guidance. Protect me from the snares of Kouzen Zaka and any negativity that seeks to turn my heart away from You. Help me to hear Your voice clearly and to respond with obedience and faithful-*

ness. May I continually seek Your presence and strength. Amen.

Prayer based on 1 Corinthians 9:24-27:

> *Lord, I run with endurance the race You have set before me. As I strive for the prize of a life in Christ, I ask for discipline and focus in my journey. Shield me from any distractions, including the approach of Kouzen Zaka, that might cause me to lose sight of my goals. Help me to train my spirit and body, dedicating my efforts to glorify You. May my life be a testimony to Your goodness and grace. Amen.*

CHAPTER THIRTY-THREE
PAPA LOKO

Papa Loko is a powerful Loa, and his importance is beautifully illustrated in a popular Haitian folk song famously performed by Toto Bissainthe: "Papa Loko ou se van, pouse n ale, nou se papiyon" (Papa Loko, you're the wind, pushing us, and we become butterflies).

As the guardian of Vodou temples (known as hounfò), he is responsible for maintaining the Vodou tradition and passing down wisdom to new initiates in the roles of Vodou priests and priestesses. He is highly respected and often honored by Vodou practitioners, who use his asson (rattle) during rituals.

But that's not all—with his extensive knowledge of herbal medicines and natural remedies, Papa Loko is also a healing Loa who can aid those in need of physical, emotional, or spiritual healing.

WARFARE PRAYER AGAINST PAPA LOKO

Father God,

In the mighty name of Jesus, I come before You, seeking and asking for Your divine protection and guidance.

I cover myself with the blood of Jesus and place my trust in You as my shield and fortress.

I stand alongside Archangel Michael, Archangel Gabriel, and the warring angels against any forces of darkness that may come my way.

I declare that no weapon formed against me shall prosper.

I take authority over every evil spirit and every plan of the enemy and declare them null and void in Jesus' name.

Lord, I ask for Your angels to come and surround me right now to guard and protect me from all harm.

Fill me with Your sword, which is Your Word, and the strength I need to stand and fight.

Grant me wisdom to discern the schemes of the enemy. Help me to stand firm in faith, knowing that You are with me.

I pray for the power of Your Word to be my sword, cutting through lies and deception, for Your Word says that it is "quick, and powerful, and sharper than any two-edged sword, piercing even to the dividing asunder of soul and spirit, and of the joints and marrow, and is a discerner of the thoughts and intents of the heart."

I declare victory over my battles today, trusting in Your promise that greater is He that is in me than he that is in the world.

In Jesus' mighty name,
Amen.

CHAPTER THIRTY-FOUR
AYIZAN VELEKETE

A wise old woman who walks the roads with her trusty cane, Ayizan Velekete is far more than a simple figure. She is the guardian of commerce and the economy, known for her ancient wisdom and pure spirit. Her benevolent gaze watches over business activities and roads, and Vodou practitioners often call upon her for success in their ventures.

As the wife of Papa Loko, she works alongside him to ensure the purity and respect of the Vodou tradition. Her favorite tree is the palm tree, a symbol of royalty, though she is often depicted as a shrewd and perceptive old woman.

WARFARE PRAYER AGAINST AYIZAN VELEKETE

Jesus,

I come before You in Your name, Jesus, seeking Your divine protection and strength. I acknowledge that I am engaged in spiritual warfare, and I rely on Your power to overcome all forms of evil.

I declare that every spirit of Ayizan Velekete that seeks to disrupt my life, my family, and my calling is bound in the name of Jesus. I apply the blood of Jesus over myself, my loved ones, and my surroundings. I decree that no weapon formed against me shall prosper, and I take authority over any negative influence or stronghold that these spirits may have.

Holy Spirit, fill me with Your wisdom and discernment as I confront these spirits. I ask for Your guidance to recognize their lies and to stand firm in my faith. I choose to walk in the light of Your truth and to follow the path You have set before me.

So, in the name of Jesus, I command any Ayizan Velekete spirit to depart from my life NOW and to return to the abyss from which it came. I thank You, Lord, for hearing my prayer and for the victory that is mine through Christ.

I pray for peace, strength, and an unyielding faith as I continue this journey in You, Lord Jesus. May Your angels encamp around me, shielding me from all harm.

Thank You, Lord, for Your unfailing love and protection. I trust in You and give You all the glory.

In Jesus' mighty name,
Amen.

CHAPTER THIRTY-FIVE
MET KAFOU

If you're brave enough to summon Met Kafou, prepare for a test of willpower, determination, and discipline. This formidable Loa is the master of dark magic and sorcery, and he does not grant his favors lightly. However, if you can prove yourself worthy, Met Kafou can bestow immense power and knowledge upon you.

But be careful: his gifts come at a steep price, and he will not hesitate to exact it. If you are willing to take the risk, proceed with caution and tread carefully, lest you fall prey to the powerful forces that lie in wait.

WARFARE PRAYER AGAINST MET KAFOU

Lord,

I come before You in the name of Jesus Christ, my Lord and Savior. I acknowledge Your supremacy and power over all darkness and evil. I seek Your protection and guidance as I confront the forces that oppose Your will.

Ephesians 6:10-12 says: "Finally, be strong in the Lord and in His mighty power. Put on the full armor of God, so that you can take your stand against the devil's schemes. For our struggle is not against flesh and blood, but against the rulers, against the authorities, against the powers of this dark world and against the spiritual forces of evil in the heavenly realms."

I declare that no weapon formed against me shall prosper (Isaiah 54:17). I plead the blood of Jesus over my life, my family, and all areas of my existence. I bind any spirits of confusion, fear, and oppression in the name of Jesus.

2 Corinthians 10:4-5 says: "The weapons we fight with are not the weapons of the world. On the contrary, they have divine power to demolish strongholds. We demolish arguments and every pretension that sets itself up against the knowledge of God, and we take captive every thought to make it obedient to Christ."

So, Lord Jesus, I take authority over every spirit that seeks to bring harm or negativity into my life. I declare that

I am a child of the Most High God, and I stand firm in His promises. I ask for Your divine protection to surround me and to lead me away from traps and snares set by the enemy.

Psalm 91:1-2 says: "He who dwells in the secret place of the Most High shall abide under the shadow of the Almighty. I will say of the Lord, 'He is my refuge and my fortress, my God, in Him I will trust.'"

I now call upon Archangels Michael and Gabriel, Your warring angels, to encamp around me (Psalm 34:7), providing strength and support as I resist the adversary. Strengthen me, Lord, in this battle, and grant me the wisdom to discern Your voice amidst the chaos, in the mighty name of Jesus Christ.

Thank You, Lord, for Your shield of love and protection. I trust and believe that You are fighting for me and that victory is already mine in Christ Jesus. I plead Your precious blood over my life and over all of my possessions.

In the mighty name of Jesus,
Amen.

CHAPTER THIRTY-SIX
ERZULIE DANTÒ

Erzulie Dantò, also known as Mami Dantò, Erzulie Dantò is a powerful and protective mother figure in the Vodou tradition. Often depicted holding a knife, she symbolizes justice and will fiercely fight to protect her children, who are her loyal followers. She is a single mother and a Haitian peasant who is fiercely independent and takes care of her own.

Unlike the Erzulie Freda deity, Dantò does not need frills or coquetry. Instead, she is strong and determined to provide for her children. Despite her harsh appearance, she is deeply caring and dedicated to her children and will stop at nothing to protect them. She is also a guardian and protector of orphans, sick children, and those who have been abused.

WARFARE PRAYER AGAINST ERZULIE DANTÒ

*Heavenly Father, I come before You in humility and
strength. I ask for Your divine protection over my life
and my loved ones. The scripture says,*

*"I will give you the keys to the kingdom of heaven, and
whatever you bind on earth shall be bound in heaven,
and whatever you loose on earth shall be loosed in
heaven" (Matthew 16:19).*

*I bind all malevolent plans and influences seeking to
disrupt my peace and happiness. I stand firm in Your
promises, knowing that no weapon formed against me
shall prosper.*

*I call upon heaven to back me up and the consuming fire
of God to be dispatched, along with archangels and
divine beings, to surround me, shielding me from any
negative energy or intentions that may arise from
Erzulie Dantò or any other spirit.*

*Lord Jesus, be a lamp unto my feet and a light to my path,
casting away shadows of fear and doubt, and filling
me with courage and resolve. Grant me wisdom,
knowledge, and understanding in my decisions, and
strengthen me to overcome every challenge.*

In Your mighty name,
Amen.

PART FIVE
TARGETED PRAYERS

Incorporating prayer into your life can enrich your spiritual walk and enhance your ability to navigate the challenges that come your way.

"Heavenly Father, encircle me with Your divine power.
Protect my spirit from forces that dwell in darkness
May no evil penetrate this sacred space. Amen."

CHAPTER THIRTY-SEVEN
PRAYERS OF PROTECTION

DEUTERONOMY 33:12

> And of Benjamin he said, The beloved of the Lord shall dwell in safety by him; and the Lord shall cover him all the day long, and he shall dwell between his shoulders.

— DEUTERONOMY 33:12

Moses, a messenger of God, gave this blessing, among others, to the children of Israel before his death. This is a reassuring verse on God's enduring presence in our daily lives.

Heavenly Father,

I come before You with a heart full of gratitude for Your

love and protection. Thank You for the promise in Deuteronomy 33:12 that speaks to the security and peace found in Your presence. Like Benjamin, may I be known as one of those who are beloved by You, wrapped in Your embrace.

Lord, I ask for Your guidance in my life. Help me to trust in Your providence and to dwell in the safety of Your care. May I find my strength in You, knowing that You are always by my side, defending me and watching over me.

Teach me to rest in the assurance that You have chosen me as Your own, and may I reflect that love to those around me. As I navigate the challenges of life, let me be a source of encouragement to others, reminding them of Your mighty right hand upon their lives.

Thank You, Lord, for the blessings You continuously shower upon us. We put our hope and trust in You, for You are our refuge and our fortress.

In Jesus' name,
Amen.

PSALM 91

 He that dwelleth in the secret place of the most High shall abide under the shadow of the Almighty. I will say of the Lord, He is my refuge and my fortress: my God; in Him will I trust.

— PSALM 91:1-2

This verse in Psalm offers us insight into how we might receive God's protection, by staying in God's company and trusting in Him.

. . .

Heavenly Father,

I come before You, seeking refuge under Your mighty wings. I declare that You are my fortress and my stronghold, the One in whom I trust. As I lift my voice in prayer, I claim the promises of Psalms 91 over my life, my ministry, my spouse, my children, my family, and all of my possessions in the name of Jesus Christ.

I thank You for covering me with Your feathers and for Your faithfulness that is my shield and rampart. No evil shall befall me, and no plague shall come near my dwelling. I stand firm in Your protection, for You have given Your angels charge over me to guard me in all my ways.

In the face of adversity, from every demons and spirits from the underground world I will not fear the terror of the night, nor the arrows that fly by day. For I know that You are with me, and Your presence brings me peace. I declare victory over any spiritual warfare that seeks to harm or hinder me, my ministry, family, job, business, children, spouse and finances and every-thing that concerns me.

I plead the blood of Jesus over my life, my family, and my circumstances. I take authority over any negativity, fear, or doubt, casting it back into the pit of hell in the name of Jesus. I stand in the assurance that You are my deliverer, rescuing me from every trap and peril.

Lord, I trust in Your salvation and declare that I will see

Your goodness in the land of the living. I will walk in faith, courage, and strength, knowing that You are my protector and guide.

Thank You for hearing my prayer Jesus as I place my life in Your hands, confident in Your promises and in your bosom.

In Jesus' name,
Amen.

2 THESSALONIANS 3:3

 But the Lord is faithful, and He will strengthen and protect you from the evil one.

— 2 THESSALONIANS 3:3

How wonderful it is that, just as we have faith in the Lord, the Lord has faith in us. He trusts that we'll bravely resist the influence of evil, and we should trust in Him to protect us in that plight.

Heavenly Father,

I come before You in the name of Jesus, standing firm on the promises found in Your Word. According to 2 Thessalonians 3:3, You are faithful and will strengthen and protect me from the evil one. I thank You for Your unwavering faithfulness in my life.

Lord, I call upon Your mighty Name for protection over my mind, body, and spirit. I ask that You surround me with Your divine hedge of protection. Cover me with Your armor, so that I may be safeguarded from every attack of the enemy.

I declare that no weapon formed against me shall prosper, and every scheme of the adversary is thwarted in the name of Jesus. Strengthen my faith and resolve, help me to stand firm in Your truth, and let me not waver in the face of trials.

I pray for my loved ones as well. Protect them and every spirits and demons from the underground world and keep them under Your wings, guiding them away from temptation and danger. Give us all the strength to persevere and remain steadfast in our walk with You.

In the Mighty name of Jesus teach our hands to war and our finger to fight against demons and spirits in the spiritual world in the name of Jesus to declare victory over the enemy that was sent against my ministry, my family, my friends, my love ones, and finances, and all of my possessions in the name of Jesus.

Thank You, Lord, for Your faithfulness and for continually working in my life. I trust in Your promises and place my battles in Your capable hands.

In Jesus' name,
Amen.

ISAIAH 41:10

 So do not fear, for I am with you; do not be dismayed,
for I am your God. I will strengthen you and help you; I
will uphold you with my righteous right hand.

— ISAIAH 41:10

This scripture from the Book of Isaiah is one of the most repeated
Bible verses, not only for its poetic beauty but also for the warmth
and comfort that it brings.

Heavenly Father,

*I come before You in faith, standing on the promise of
Isaiah 41:10, where You remind us not to fear, for You
are with us. I declare that I am not dismayed, for You
are my God. Thank You for strengthening me, helping
me, and upholding me with Your righteous right
hand.*

*Lord, I ask for Your protection over my life, ministry and
my loved ones. I release the fire of God and Surround
us with Your angels as I face the battles that come my
way. Equip me with strength and courage to confront
every challenge, knowing that You are by my side, just
like you led the Moses and the Israelites by a cloud by
day and a pillar of fire by night in the name of Jesus.*

*In the name of Jesus, I cast out fear, anxiety, and doubt
and unbelief and I replace them with Your peace and
assurance. Help me to stand firm in faith, trusting in*

Your providence and power. May I always remember
that You are my refuge and fortress in times of
trouble.

Thank You for fighting my battles and giving me victory. I
claim the promise that You will never leave nor
forsake me. I am more than a conqueror through
Christ who strengthens me. Thank You, Jesus!

In Jesus' name,
Amen.

PSALM 121:5-8

The Lord watches over you — the Lord is your shade at
your right hand; the sun will not harm you by day, nor
the moon by night. The Lord will keep you from all
harm — he will watch over your life; the Lord will
watch over your coming and going both now and
forevermore.

— PSALM 121:5-8

This Psalm reminds us that we can always trust in the knowledge
that the Lord is watching over us. He will never leave us alone, and
He will protect us.

Abba Father,

I come before You, declaring that You are my keeper and
my protector. Your Word assures me that You watch
over me, like a shepherd watching his flock. I thank

*You for being my shade and my refuge, shielding me
from the trials and tribulations of life.*

*In times of warfare, whether physical, spiritual, or
emotional, I proclaim that You are the One who keeps
my foot from slipping. I ask for Your divine protection
over my life, my loved ones, and all that concerns me.
Cover me with Your wings, and let Your angels
encamp around me, guarding me in all my ways.*

*Lord, I trust that You will preserve me from evil.
Strengthen my heart and mind to stand firm against
the adversary. I declare that nothing can come against
me when You are my defender. I plead the blood of
Jesus over every aspect of my life, knowing that You
are my strength and stronghold.*

*May Your presence guide me today and every day,
bringing me peace as I walk in faith. I claim victory
through Your mighty name, knowing that You are my
faithful protector from this time forth and forevermore. Amen and Amen.*

*In Jesus' name,
Amen.*

PSALM 18:2-3

The Lord is my rock and my fortress and my savior, My
God, my rock, in whom I take refuge; My shield and
the horn of my salvation, my stronghold. I call upon
the Lord, who is worthy to be praised, And I am saved
from my enemies.

— PSALM 18:2-3

When your problems seem insurmountable and your fate sealed, remember David, who was saved from certain death by the hands of Saul.

My God of War,

I come before You today, declaring that You are my rock
and my fortress. In times of trouble, I find refuge in
You, trusting in Your mighty power to protect and
deliver me. I thank You for being my shield, guarding
my heart and soul against every attack and schemes
from spirits and demons from the underground world.

Lord, I call upon You, for You are worthy of all my praise. I
seek Your strength and guidance as I face challenges
and adversities. Surround me with Your divine
protection, and let Archangel Micheal and warring
angels to be my defenders against all forms of evil.

I declare victory over all my enemies, both seen and
unseen, knowing that with You on my side, I shall not
be shaken or moved, Empower me with courage and
faith as I stand firm in Your promises because you are
the God that answers by fire.

Thank You, Lord, for being my stronghold. I place my trust
in You and rejoice in the salvation You provide.

Hallelujah!

I thank You, Jesus for answering my prayers.

In Jesus' mighty Name,
Amen.

JUDE 1:20-25

But you, dear friends, by building yourselves up in your most holy faith and praying in the Holy Spirit, keep yourselves in God's love as you wait for the mercy of our Lord Jesus Christ to bring you to eternal life.

Be merciful to those who doubt; save others by snatching them from the fire; to others show mercy, mixed with fear—hating even the clothing stained by corrupted flesh.

To him who is able to keep you from stumbling and to present you before his glorious pres-ence without fault and with great joy— to the only God our Savior be glory, majesty, power and authority, through Jesus Christ our Lord, before all ages, now and forevermore! Amen.

— JUDE 1:20-25

In the mighty name of Jesus Christ,

I come before You, Lord, standing firm on Your promises of protection and deliverance. I declare: "Every satanic attack against my life, scatter by fire, in the name of Jesus." I believe in Your power to break every chain of the enemy and to set me free from every form of spiri-tual bondage.

Lord Jesus, as written in verses 20–25, I build myself up in my most holy faith, praying in the Holy Spirit. Keep me in Your love as I await the mercy of our Lord Jesus Christ that leads to eternal life. I trust in Your promise to keep me from falling and to present me faultless before the presence of Your glory with exceeding joy.

I call forth Archangel Michael and the warring angels to fight on my behalf against the forces of darkness from the underworld, in the name of Jesus. I cover myself with the full armor of God, for I know, according to Ephesians 6:12, that we wrestle not against flesh and blood, but against principalities, powers, rulers of the darkness of this world, and spiritual wickedness in high places. Lord Jesus, as I war against these forces, let them encounter Your consuming fire that burns away everything that is not of You.

I rebuke every strategy of the enemy aimed at my life, my family, and my destiny. Let Your fire consume every plan of darkness, and may Your light dispel every shadow of evil. I declare victory over every satanic oppression, knowing that greater is He who is in me than he who is in the world.

Clothe me in Your armor so that I may stand firm against the wiles of the devil. Surround me with Your hedge of protection, and let Your angels encamp around me. I put my trust in You, Lord, knowing that You are my fortress, my deliverer, and my shield.

In Jesus' mighty Name,
Amen.

ADDITIONAL SCRIPTURES OF PROTECTION

Here are some additional scriptures that you can pray for protection:

- *James 4:7*: "Submit yourselves, then, to God. Resist the devil, and he will flee from you."
- *Ephesians 3:12*: "In whom we have boldness and access with confidence through our faith in him."
- *2 Corinthians 3:12*: "Since we have such a hope, we are very bold."
- *2 Timothy 1:6-7*: God gives us a spirit of boldness, power, love, and self-discipline to identify and develop our gifts.
- *2 Corinthians 7:4*: Paul tells the Corinthians that he is able to speak to them with great openness and boldness.
- *Ezra 7:28*: "I took courage, for the hand of the Lord my God was on me."
- *Luke 11:8*: The NIV renders this verse as "shameless audacity," so I thank you Jesus that now am walking into the spirit of boldness nothing shall by any means hold me back Amen.

DECLARATIONS AND AFFIRMATIONS OF PROTECTION

- I am protected by the power of Jesus' name, and no weapon formed against me shall prosper.
- I walk in victory over satanic attacks, as I am covered by the blood of Jesus.
- God's fire guards my life, scattering every plan of the enemy.
- I release the Arch Angel Micheal, my warring angel, to stand with me and fight in Jesus' Mighty Name.

CHAPTER THIRTY-EIGHT
PRAYERS FOR DELIVERANCE

PSALM 34:17

> " When the righteous cry for help, the LORD hears and
> delivers them out of all their troubles.

> PSALMS 34:17

This verse can be a powerful basis for a prayer for warfare or
protection. Here's a prayer inspired by this scripture:

Jesus,

> *I'm grateful for Your compassionate love and protection. I*
> *stand on the truth of Psalm 34:17, knowing that as the*
> *righteous cry out, You hear us and deliver us from all*
> *our troubles.*

> *Lord, I ask for Your mighty hand to be with me and my*

ministry and my loved ones in times of battle and strife. Shield us from demons and spirits from the underground world and surround us with Your angels. Give us strength and courage to face the challenges before us day by day that we may always remember that we do not fight alone, for You are our defender and refuge.

As I cry out to You today, I trust that You will hear my voice and grant me deliverance from any harm, oppression, or fear from demons and spirits, and equip me with wisdom and discernment as I navigate through the warfare in my life by your Holy Spirit.

Thank You, Lord, for Your promises and the assurance of Your presence. I place my full faith in You, knowing that You are greater than any challenge I may face.

In Jesus' name,
Amen.

PSALM 50:15

 And call upon me in the day of trouble; I will deliver you, and you shall glorify me.

— PSALM 50:15

Father,

In the name of Jesus, I call upon your Powerful name, Jehovah Elgabor to fight on my behalf and deliver me from those that oppress and rise up against me. I uproot every demonic interference that is trying to destroy my ministry, my husband/wife, my children, my finances, my family, my home, deliver me oh God out of the hands of the wicked that you may be glorified.

In Jesus' name,
Amen.

PSALM 34:17

 When the righteous cry for help, the LORD hears and delivers them out of all their troubles.

— PSALM 34:17

Lord Jesus,

I am your righteous and I cry out for help. I need you more than ever, and I ask that you will send Archangel Micheal and Gabriel with arrows of flaming fire to destroy every works, snare, plot, arrow and traps from demons from the underground world and deliver me oh Lord from all of them that are troubling me.

Thank you Lord for deliverance and I decree and declare victory.

In Jesus' name,
Amen.

ADDITIONAL SCRIPTURES OF PROTECTION

- *Psalm 91:1-16:* "A promise of deliverance from evil through divine reason and law."
- *Psalm 59:1-2:* "Deliver me from my enemies, O God; protect me from those who rise up against me. Deliver me from evildoers and save me from bloodthirsty men."
- *John 8:32:* "If you abide in my word, you are my disciples indeed. And you shall know the truth, and the truth shall make you free."
- *1 Corinthians 10:13:* "The Lord can help you escape difficult situations, especially temptation, if you pray to Him."
- *Philippians 4:6-7:* "Do not be anxious about anything, but in every situation, by prayer and petition, with thanksgiving, present your requests to God."
- *James 5:16:* "Therefore confess your sins to each other and pray for each other so that you may be healed. The prayer of a righteous person is powerful and effective."

CHAPTER THIRTY-NINE
PRAYERS AGAINST FEAR

2 TIMOTHY 1:7

 For God has not given us a spirit of fear, but one of power, love, and sound judgment.

— 2 TIMOTHY 1:7

In the mighty Name of Jesus,

I renounce you, spirit of fear! God has not given me the spirit of fear, but of power, love, and a sound mind. You shall no longer bind my heart or control my thoughts. I call forth the fire of God to shine upon me and dispel every shadow of fear, in the mighty name of Jesus.

Lord, as I come before You, I lay my fears and anxieties at Your feet. Help me overcome every doubt and fear that tries to rise within me. When I feel crushed by my enemies, remind me that You are a powerful and faithful God. Remind me that I can trust in You completely. I know I cannot do this on my own—I need You, Lord.

You have commanded us not to fear, for You are with us; You will strengthen us, help us, and uphold us with Your righteous right hand (Isaiah 41:10).

Therefore, I cast all my anxieties on You, because You care for me (1 Peter 5:7).

Now, in the name of Jesus Christ, I put on the spirit of boldness, for Your Word commands me to be bold and courageous.

In Jesus' mighty name,
Amen.

PROVERBS 28:1

 The wicked flee when no one pursues, but the righteous are bold as a lion.

— PROVERBS 28:1

Heavenly Father,

I come before You in the name of Jesus Christ, and I thank You for your Word that guides my path. Today, I stand against any spirit of fear, deceit, and wickedness that seeks to lead me away from Your truth. I declare that the way of the guilty will not prosper in my life, and I reject any schemes of the enemy that aim to corrupt my heart or lead me astray.

Lord, I ask for Your protection over my thoughts, my actions, and my relationships. Help me to walk in righteousness and integrity, reflecting the conduct of the innocent. Give me discernment to recognize any deceptive tactics that may try to enter my mind or influence my decisions.

I pray that You expose every hidden thing and bring to light any areas of my life that need Your cleansing power. Fill me with Your truth and guide me to live a life that honors You in every way.

Thank You for Your faithfulness and for hearing my prayer. I claim victory over all deceit and darkness in my life, and I choose to stand firm in Your light.

In Jesus' name,
Amen.

CHAPTER FORTY
PRAYERS FOR PURIFICATION

JOHN 3:5

> Truly, truly, I say to you, unless one is born of water and the Spirit, he cannot enter the kingdom of God.

— JOHN 3:5

Heavenly Father,

I come before You seeking purification, Lord. Trusting in You, we echo the prayer of Isaiah: "But now, O Lord, You are our Father; we are the clay, and You our potter; and we all are the work of Your hand" (Isaiah 64:8).

May Your Holy Spirit fill me with strength and grace, banishing all darkness from my soul in the mighty name of Jesus. I ask that You cleanse my spirit from sin and purge every evil influence from my mind. Make me clean and whole again so that I may draw closer to You and experience the fullness of Your divine power.

God, please help me to turn away from sin and wrongdoing. Give my heart a desire to do good, to walk in love and friendship, and to help those around me. Protect me from every form of evil and keep me pure in Your presence.

In Jesus' name,
Amen.

MALACHI 3:3

 He will sit as a refiner and purifier of silver, and He will purify the sons of Levi and refine them like gold and silver.

— MALACHI 3:3

Heavenly Father,

You are the Refiner of my soul and the Keeper of all truth. I come to You humbly, asking You to purify me with the fire of Your holiness.

Burn away every impure thought, hidden motive, and unclean desire. Search me, O God, and know my heart; test me and know my anxious thoughts. See if there is any offensive way in me, and lead me in the way everlasting (Psalm 139:23–24).

Cleanse my body, soul, and spirit with the fire of Your truth and the washing of Your Word. Let no residue of sin remain. I declare that I belong to You, Lord. Seal me for Your glory and set me apart for righteousness.

In the mighty name of Jesus,
Amen.

PSALM 119:9

 How can a young man keep his way pure? By guarding it according to Your word.

— PSALM 119:9

Lord God Almighty,

I come to You needing to be washed clean—not just outwardly, but deep within. Let Your living Word cleanse every corner of my heart.

Remove the stains of bitterness, pride, and compromise. Renew in me a steadfast spirit, and create in me a clean heart, O God (Psalm 51:10).

Saturate me with Your presence, Holy Spirit, and guard my heart from the pollution of the world.

Wash me until I reflect Your light and truth. May my thoughts, speech, and actions be purified and pleasing to You.

Keep me in Your will, protected from deception and drawn
closer to You daily.

In Jesus' holy name,
Amen.

PART SIX
ANCHORED IN PRAYER

In times of spiritual warfare, prayer is more than a practice—it is a lifeline that keeps believers grounded, focused, and fortified.

This section reveals how living a prayer-centered life equips you to withstand and overcome the pressures of spiritual opposition. You'll discover the power of a consistent prayer lifestyle that keeps you attuned to God's voice, the depth of fasting that sharpens your spiritual sensitivity and releases breakthrough, and the unmatched strength found in praying alongside other believers in unity and purpose. Whether in private devotion or corporate gatherings, these expressions of prayer build spiritual endurance and deepen your intimacy with the Lord.

As you engage with each chapter, you'll be reminded that victory is not found in isolated moments of prayer but in a life anchored by it —firm, unshakable, and aligned with heaven's agenda.

CHAPTER FORTY-ONE

THE POWER OF A LIFESTYLE OF PRAYER

Consistency and intentionality in your practices will cultivate a deeper connection with God and strengthen your spiritual resilience. Here are some practical steps you can implement:

1. *Morning Prayer and Affirmation*

- Start your day with prayer, dedicating the day to God. Ask for guidance, strength, and protection. Consider using affirmations that reinforce your faith and remind you of God's promises.

2. *Scripture Reading*

- Incorporate reading verses that focus on spiritual warfare into your daily routine. Passages like Ephesians 6:10-18 or 2 Corinthians 10:3-5 can be particularly encouraging.

3. *Mindful Prayers Throughout the Day*

- Create moments of prayer during various activities. Whether at work, while commuting, or during breaks, take a moment to pray, thanking God or asking for assistance.

4. *Praying with Purpose*

- Make a list of specific areas where you feel spiritual battles are occurring in your life. Pray intentionally for these areas, asking for wisdom to navigate challenges and for protection.

5. *Incorporate Fasting and Prayer*

- Consider setting aside specific times for fasting coupled with prayer. This can help deepen your spiritual focus and bring clarity to the struggles you face.

6. *Use Worship Music*

- Listening to and singing worship songs can be a form of prayer. Music has the power to uplift and can serve as a reminder of God's presence in times of spiritual warfare.

7. *Prayer Partner or Group*

- Connect with others who can pray with you. Having a prayer partner or group can provide support, encouragement, and accountability in your spiritual journey.

8. *Evening Reflection and Prayer*

- Conclude your day with a time of reflection. Assess your day, offer gratitude for the positives, and pray for forgiveness and strength in areas where you struggled.

9. *Pray with Scripture*

- Turn verses into prayers. For example, you can take a verse like Psalm 144:1 and pray for God to teach you to be a warrior in His service.

10. *Journaling Your Prayers*

- Keep a prayer journal where you can write down your thoughts, prayers, and any insights you receive. This can help you see God's faithfulness over time and keep you focused.

11. *Visual Reminders*

- Place scriptures or prayer prompts around your home or workspace as reminders to pray throughout the day

12. *Engage in Acts of Service*

- Commit to serving others in your community. Acts of kindness can be a form of spiritual warfare, pushing back against negativity and spreading light.

13. *Create a Prayer Center*

- Set up a dedicated space in your home for prayer. I remember when I first started praying, I was in my bedroom on the floor. However, I wanted a more sacred space, so I took all of my shoes out of my closet and spread a blanket in there along with my Bible and my prayers. As the Holy Spirit led me to write, I would pray them daily, adding more over time, along with other items that helped me focus.

Remember— spiritual warfare is real, and prayer is a vital component in standing firm against it.

CHAPTER FORTY-TWO

THE POWER OF FASTING & PRAYER

Fasting has long been a practice in many spiritual traditions, particularly in the context of prayer and spiritual warfare. It is often seen as a powerful tool for deepening one's connection with the divine, seeking clarity, and cultivating strength during challenging times. Here are some insights into the importance of fasting in spiritual warfare, along with suggestions on how to incorporate it into your prayer life.

1. *Spiritual Clarity*

Fasting can help clear the mind and spirit, allowing you to focus more intently on prayer and seeking God's guidance. It diminishes distractions, making it easier to hear spiritual truths and insights.

2. *Humility and Dependence*

By fasting, you acknowledge your dependence on God rather

than on physical sustenance. This act of humility can bring you closer to God and reinforce your faith.

3. *Strengthening Prayer*

Fasting is often combined with prayer in many religious texts and practices. The two together can create a more potent form of intercession, as fasting is seen as a way to deepen your communication with God.

4. *Spiritual Warfare*

Many believers view fasting as a means to combat spiritual attacks. By denying the body, you may find increased strength in your spiritual life, enabling you to resist temptations and confront challenges more effectively.

5. *Manifesting Intentions*

Fasting can be a way to demonstrate your commitment to specific intentions or prayers. It can act as a physical manifestation of your spiritual hunger and desire for change.

INCORPORATING FASTING INTO YOUR PRAYER LIFE

Here are some practical steps you can take to incorporate fasting into your prayer life.

1. *Set Clear Intentions*

Before beginning a fast, clarify what you're praying for or seeking. This can be guidance, strength, or the resolution of specific challenges. When I pray, I always ask Jesus how He wants me to fast for a specific person or preaching engagement. However, I basically fast for spiritual growth daily.

2. *Choose a Fasting Method*

There are various ways to fast, from complete fasts (abstaining from all food and drink) to partial fasts (skipping certain meals or certain types of food). Choose a method that feels right for you and aligns with your health.

3. *Create a Prayer Schedule*

Designate specific times for prayer during your fasting period. This can help you remain focused and intentional about your communication with God.

4. *Incorporate Scripture*

Use scripture passages related to fasting and spiritual warfare to guide your prayers. Reading and meditating on biblical texts can enhance your experience.

5. *Journal Your Thoughts*

Keep a journal during your fasting. Write down your prayers, insights, and any revelations you receive. This can help you track your spiritual growth and process your experiences.

I remember when the Lord started talking and showing me so much. I didn't fully understand what was going on in my life as a born-again believer, so I went to my dad one day and told him what I was experiencing. My dad instructed me to buy a book and a pen and write down everything that the Lord was showing me and telling me. It helped me so much.

May I tell you that sometimes the Lord will give you His revelation like a puzzle—a little here and a little there. This is why it is so important to keep a journal and a pen on you at all times. When the Holy Spirit speaks, jot down everything He says to you.

6. *Community Support*

If appropriate, involve others in your fasting practice. This could be done through group prayer sessions or shared experiences, fostering encouragement and support.

7. *Reflect Post-Fast*

After completing your fast, take time to reflect on the experience. Consider what you learned and how you felt throughout the process. This reflection can enhance your future fasting practices.

8. *Practice Gratitude*

At the end of your fasting period, take time to express gratitude for what you've learned and experienced. This can reinforce the spiritual benefits of the practice.

Integrating fasting into your prayer life can be a profound way to enhance your spiritual journey, particularly in times of struggle or when seeking deeper understanding and connection with God and His word.

PERSONAL EXPERIENCES WITH FASTING & PRAYER

My experience in ministry under my spiritual leader during services was a great adventure for me. I always took the experience as my training ground. Learning in every area of ministry can become challenging but also helpful. The more I served as a servant of God, the more I learned—from watching my leader fast and pray for healing and deliverance, to receiving 911 calls from persons who were demonized and homes experiencing paranormal activities, to people vacating newly built buildings, and also during prophetic services where witches and warlocks would come and try to interrupt services.

I have seen many people come into the ministry and fall down dead with no sign of life. During my training, I watched as my leader would lay hands on them, and we prayed until we saw signs of life return to their bodies. There were times when my leader would send me to deal with other persons during healing and deliverance and casting out demons. Now, by the Spirit of God, alongside my husband in our ministry in Madison, Wisconsin, I am doing the very same thing in healing and deliverance.

CHAPTER FORTY-THREE
THE POWER OF CORPORATE PRAYER

While personal prayer is vital to building your spiritual strength, there is a unique and powerful anointing released when believers gather together in unity to seek the Lord. Community prayer is a divine weapon—one that amplifies faith, multiplies agreement, and invites the supernatural presence of God into a region, home, or situation.

> For where two or three are gathered together in My name, I am there in the midst of them.
>
> — MATTHEW 18:20

When the body of Christ comes together with one voice, one mind, and one purpose, the spiritual atmosphere shifts. Chains are broken. Walls come down. God moves swiftly in environments where there is unity, humility, and expectation.

Whether you are part of a local church, ministry group, or just a few faithful believers, corporate prayer is essential for spiritual protection, revival, and breakthrough. It is one of the most effective ways to build a strong spiritual foundation—not just for yourself, but for your entire community. There is strength in numbers—especially in the Spirit. When a group of Believers comes together in agreement, heaven responds.

- Collective prayer covers more ground and invites a greater level of angelic assistance.
- It strengthens intercessors who may be weary from fighting alone.
- It opens the door for prophetic revelation, healing, and corporate deliverance.

In Scripture, we see many examples where community prayer led to supernatural results:

- The early church gathered constantly to pray, resulting in miracles, deliverance, and growth (Acts 2:42–47).
- Peter was released from prison as the church prayed earnestly on his behalf (Acts 12:5–11).
- Jehoshaphat and the people of Judah fasted and prayed together, and the Lord delivered them from their enemies without a sword being raised (2 Chronicles 20:3–22).

These moments remind us that we are stronger together, especially when we lift up one another and war in unity. Therefore, if you feel led to initiate or strengthen a community prayer movement, here are some steps to help you get started:

1. *Set the Spiritual Intent*

Begin with a clear purpose. Is the gathering for warfare? Intercession? Healing? Restoration? Make the focus known and keep Christ at the center.

2. *Cover It in Prayer*

Before inviting others, spend time personally praying over the gathering. Ask the Holy Spirit to guide, protect, and lead the agenda.

3. *Choose a Time and Place Conducive to Unity*

It could be in a home, a church, outdoors, or even online. Choose a space where people can focus and be free to worship and pray without distraction.

4. *Appoint Intercessors or Prayer Leaders*

Consider inviting trusted believers to help lead portions of the prayer. They can focus on specific themes such as families, regions, deliverance, or healing.

5. *Incorporate Scripture and Worship*

Begin with reading the Word or singing worship songs to invite God's presence. Scripture-based prayers create a strong foundation and keep the atmosphere aligned with truth.

6. *Allow Room for the Holy Spirit to Move*

Don't script everything. Be sensitive to shifts in the room and allow spontaneous worship, prophecy, or deliverance to happen if God begins to move.

7. *Pray for Protection and Closure*

Always end the gathering by sealing the atmosphere in prayer, pleading the blood of Jesus over everyone present, and declaring that every assignment of retaliation is null and void.

8. *Accessibility*

Make sure the venue is accessible for all participants, including those with disabilities.

9. *Follow-Up: Create a Support Network*

After the gathering, consider establishing a group or network for continued support, where participants can share prayers, updates, and organize future meetings, such as WhatsApp groups.

10. *Feedback*

Encourage attendees to provide feedback on the event to improve future gatherings.

11. *Additional Activities*

Regular Meetings: Consider making the prayer gathering a recurring event for ongoing support and community bonding, such as meeting for prayer and coffee or even at the ministry, park, or beach.

Workshops or Discussions: Host additional events focused on spiritual growth, mental wellness, or community service to strengthen bonds.

By focusing on community, spirituality, and collective intention, these gatherings can provide a nurturing environment that promotes healing and resilience.

PART SEVEN
RESOURCES
FOR GROWTH

Spiritual growth doesn't end when the battle quiets—it deepens through continued support, reflection, and intentional connection with God.

This final section offers tools to help you stay grounded, including encouragement for building a sustaining support system and a closing prayer to seal the journey in faith. Whether you're coming out of warfare or stepping into a new season, these resources are designed to nourish your spirit and equip you for lasting transformation.

CHAPTER FORTY-FOUR

SUPPORT THAT SUSTAINS

Spiritual warfare is not a one-time event but a lifelong journey of discernment, discipline, and devotion. After engaging in deep prayer and breaking strongholds, it is important to stay rooted, informed, and supported. This chapter offers resources and guidance to help you grow spiritually, remain protected, and continue walking in victory.

BOOKS AND LITERATURE

As you continue your pursuit of deliverance and discernment, reading materials grounded in biblical truth can strengthen your understanding of the spiritual realm.

- *Recommended Readings:* Seek out books that explore spiritual warfare, biblical authority, and the power of prayer. Look for authors who operate with integrity, sound doctrine, and sensitivity to the Holy Spirit.

- *Classic Texts:* Consider studying foundational works on spirituality and demonology, including writings from renowned revivalists, theologians, and intercessors who have walked deeply with God. These resources can provide historical insight and practical instruction to sharpen your discernment.

> My people are destroyed for lack of knowledge.
>
> — HOSEA 4:6

Equip yourself with wisdom to stay vigilant and spiritually aware.

ONLINE RESOURCES

The digital age has made it easier than ever to find spiritual support and community, no matter where you are in the world.

- *Websites and Forums*: There are biblically grounded websites and online forums where believers share testimonies, prayer requests, and deliverance teachings. Use discretion and always test the spirit behind the content (1 John 4:1).

- *Online Prayer Groups*: Joining virtual prayer groups or intercessory Zoom calls can offer accountability, encouragement, and collective power. These communities are especially beneficial for those without a strong local church or ministry connection.

Remember, technology can be a tool for warfare when it is consecrated and used to glorify God.

SPIRITUAL ADVISORS AND COUNSELORS

No warrior fights alone. God often uses trusted leaders and mentors to guide us through battles, offer wisdom, and help us discern God's voice.

- *Finding Spiritual Guidance:* Seek out pastors, counselors, or deliverance ministers who are Spirit-led, biblically sound, and submitted to godly leadership themselves. Ask the Holy Spirit to lead you to those with pure hearts and clean hands.

- *The Role of Mentorship:* A spiritual advisor can walk with you through seasons of warfare, provide covering, and help you grow in your gifts. Proverbs 11:14 reminds us: *"Where there is no counsel, the people fall; but in the multitude of counselors there is safety."*

Do not isolate yourself. Healing, growth, and deliverance often come through safe spiritual relationships.

The journey of spiritual warfare through prayer is a holy calling—one that requires faith, courage, wisdom, and community. By embracing the strategies and prayers in this book, you are stepping into a divine assignment: to confront and destroy the influence of underground demonic forces and release the freedom of God's kingdom here on earth.

Let this book serve as a sword in your hand and a light in your path. Whether you are praying over your family, leading a ministry, hosting a crusade, or crying out for revival in the End-Time, know that heaven is backing you.

Approach every battle with reverence. Respect the unseen realm.

And most of all, seek the guidance of the Holy Spirit, who will teach you how to pray, how to discern, and how to move in authority.

May you walk in boldness. May your prayers carry weight. And may your life bear witness to the power and victory of Jesus Christ.

CHAPTER FORTY-FIVE

CLOSING PRAYER

Heavenly Father,

I pray for the person reading this book. I pray that You cover them and all their possessions under the Blood of Jesus, and that You release reinforcements of Your angels to fight on their behalf.

I pray, dear Jesus, that this book will come alive in their lives, open their eyes to Your supernatural divine wisdom, knowledge, and understanding, and grant them an outpouring of Your revelation on targeted prayers to destroy demons from the underground world.

I also pray for the person who is a forerunner in ministry, that this book will bring about a drastic change and turnaround, reigniting Your fire within their ministry to restore the Apostolic movement in the church, moving through the demonstration of Your Holy

Spirit with signs, wonders, and miracles, and the breaker's anointing to destroy yokes and lift the burdens of Your people.

God, we know that You are waiting, as stated in Romans 8:22, where Your Word says, "For we know that the whole creation has been groaning together in the pains of childbirth until now."

So, we thank You, Jesus, and we will allow Your will to be done on earth as it is in heaven.

In Jesus Name,
Amen.

ACKNOWLEDGMENTS

I want to personally thank my husband, *Apostle Robin Mielke*, for always praying for me and encouraging me to find a quiet place to write whatever God placed on my heart. Your love, patience, and spiritual support have meant more than words can express.

A special thank you to my spiritual mother, *Apostle Dinah Knowles,* for pushing me into the things of God and stirring me in the right direction. Your guidance and wisdom have been a blessing on my journey.

To my *praying sisters in Christ*, who have stood by me from day one of Divine Connection—thank you for always having my back. I love you all dearly.

And to everyone who has been praying me through this process, I could not have done it without you. Your prayers have carried me, and for that, I offer my deepest gratitude.

ABOUT THE AUTHOR

Apostle Staria Mielke is a devoted servant of Jesus Christ, inspired by this book to press even further in her calling to serve Him as Lord and Savior. She is blessed to be married to her husband, Apostle Robin Mielke, and together they are the proud parents of six beautiful children.

Chosen by God and handpicked from her mother's womb to fulfill His divine assignments, Apostle Staria's life has been marked by purpose and obedience. She was born and raised on the beautiful island of Andros in the Bahamas, where her spiritual journey began. At the age of 30, she officially entered ministry, serving faithfully under the mentorship of a powerful shepherd who trained and equipped her in every area of ministry—including healing and deliverance.

Today, Apostle Staria walks boldly in her calling as God continues to use her mightily. Truly, her tongue is as *"the pen of a ready writer"* (Psalm 45:1), declaring His glory to the nations.

www.ingramcontent.com/pod-product-compliance
Lightning Source LLC
Chambersburg PA
CBHW051507120626
46551CB00012B/818